Interdisciplinary Illumination: Unveiling Uncharted Research Paths

{Peer Reviewed}

Editors

Dr. R. K. Saran

Dr. Umamah Mufti

Dr. M. Sasirekhamani

NOTION PRESS

2024

NOTION PRESS

India. Singapore. Malaysia.

Published by: Notion Press

Publication Year: July, 2024

Editors: Dr. R. K. Saran, Dr. Umamah mufti, Dr. M. Sasirekhamani

Made with ❤ on the Notion Press Platform.

www.notionpress.com

Contents

Preface

The rapid advancement of science and technology in the 21st century has opened up a plethora of new research avenues, many of which lie at the intersection of traditional disciplines. This edited volume, "Interdisciplinary Illumination: Unveiling Uncharted Research Paths," seeks to explore these emerging frontiers by bringing together a diverse array of perspectives from various fields. Our goal is to foster a deeper understanding of how interdisciplinary approaches can lead to groundbreaking discoveries and innovative solutions to complex problems. In this book, we present a collection of chapters written by leading experts and pioneering researchers who have embraced the interdisciplinary ethos. These contributions span a wide range of topics, from the convergence of biology and nanotechnology to the integration of environmental science with social sciences. By highlighting the synergies between distinct fields, we aim to showcase the transformative potential of interdisciplinary research. This volume is structured to guide readers through the diverse landscape of interdisciplinary research. Each chapter offers insights into the unique methodologies employed, the challenges encountered, and the significant findings achieved. Moreover, we have included discussions on the practical implications of these studies, illustrating how interdisciplinary approaches can address real-world issues in innovative ways. We hope that this book will serve as a valuable resource for researchers, practitioners, and students who are eager to explore new research paths and contribute to the evolving tapestry of knowledge. By illuminating the potential of interdisciplinary research, we aspire to inspire a new generation of scholars to venture beyond conventional boundaries and embark on journeys of discovery that will shape the future of science and society.

It is our sincere hope that "Interdisciplinary Illumination: Unveiling Uncharted Research Paths" will not only inform but also inspire, encouraging readers to embrace the interdisciplinary approach and explore the uncharted territories of research with curiosity, creativity, and an open mind.

Warm regards,

Editors

Dr. R.K. Saran

Dr. Umamah Mufti

Dr. M. Sasirekhamani

Dr. Radha Kishan Saran (Dr. R.K. Saran), is Research Representative and working as research fellow in Department of Microbiology, Maharaja Ganga Singh University, Bikaner. He has completed his doctoral degree from Department of Environmental Science, Maharaja Ganga Singh University, Bikaner. His expertise in microbiology and geospatial technology in recent years has risen him up in academics and research. He holds postgraduate degrees in Environmental science, Geography and Economics. He has several publications including research paper in International and National journals, UGC Care listed / Web of Science/ Scopes/ Journals and chapters in ISBN books.

Books Edited:

- **Bridging Boundaries: Exploring Interdisciplinary Research: Dr. R. K. Saran**, Meha Khiria and Surendar Thori, NOTION PRESS, India. Singapore. Malaysia, Published by Notion Press 2023, ISBN-13: 979-889133167-9
- **Societal Synthesis: A Holistic Approach to Research, Dr. E. Jayantakumar Singh, Dr. R. K. Saran, Dr. K. K. Chandel**, NOTION PRESS, India. Singapore. Malaysia, Published by Notion Press 2024, ISBN-13: **979-889415650-7.**
- **Interwoven Narratives: Uniting Diverse Perspectives, Dr. Manjula A. C., Dr. Ramakrishna Bagguri, Dr. R.K. Saran**, NOTION PRESS, India. Singapore. Malaysia, Published by Notion Press 2024, ISBN-13: **979-889322502-0.**
- **Innovative Insights: Interdisciplinary Research Breakthroughs, Dr. R. K. Saran, Dr. Keshavamurthy M. and Vinay Raikwar**, NOTION PRESS, India. Singapore. Malaysia, Published by Notion Press 2023, ISBN-13: **979-889186101-5.**

Dr. M. Sasirekhamani serves as an Assistant Professor in the Department of Biotechnology at Thulasi College of Arts and Science, Thoothukudi. Her scholarly pursuits and research contributions have significantly advanced the fields of biotechnology, food technology, and marine biotechnology. Renowned for her expertise, she delves into the application of cutting-edge biological techniques and explores innovative solutions for enhancing food security and sustainability. Her academic journey is marked by a profound dedication to the latest developments in nanoparticle research, reflecting her commitment to scientific excellence. Dr. Sasirekhamani's work extends to collaborative projects with international researchers, further amplifying the impact of her research on global scientific communities. Her dedication to teaching and mentoring the next generation of scientists underscores her holistic approach to academia, combining research, education, and practical application to address some of the most pressing challenges in biotechnology today.

Dr. Umamah Mufti holds a Ph.D. in Environmental Sciences, a Bachelor's in Biosciences (Hons) from Jamia Millia Islamia, a Master's in Environmental Sciences from the University of Delhi, and an M.Phil. from JNU. She has extensive training in GIS, Remote Sensing, HPLC, and AAS. With over 10 years of experience, she is the Deputy Director at The Lakshya- A Society for Social and Environmental Development, and has previously worked as an Environmental Educator and Analyst at Alset Renewables. She has completed various postgraduate diplomas in Environment and Sustainable Development, Urban Planning, Disaster Management, Computer Applications, Business Accounting, and International Environmental Law. Her research sustainable development, carbon sequestration, green technology, climate change, and disaster risk mitigation, with active involvement in studying the mental health impacts of COVID-19, sleep patterns, and their environmental links. Dr. Mufti, a recipient of the 10th Delhi Rattan Award 2024, has published numerous articles on the pandemic's impact on the environment and human health, and has received multiple awards for her academic and professional contributions.

1. Unlocking Nature's Potential in Carbon Sequestration by Terrestrial, Aquatic and Marine Ecosystems

Keshavamurthy M[1], Bhoomika A[2], Shankara S[3], Srinivasulu M. V*[4].

[1,2]*Department of Life Sciences, Acharya Bangalore B-School, Bengaluru -560 091, Karnataka, India.*

[3]*Department of Microbiology, Govt. Science College, Nrupathunga University, Bengaluru – 560 001, Karnataka, India.*

[*4]*Department of Botany, Govt. Science College, Nrupathunga University, Bengaluru – 560 001, Karnataka, India.*

Authors details

[1]Dr. Keshavamurthy M, Assistant Professor and Head, Department of Life Sciences, Acharya Bangalore B-School, Bengaluru - 560 091, Karnataka, India.

[3]Dr.Shankara S., Associate Professor, Department of Microbiology, Govt. Science College, Nrupathunga University, Bengaluru – 560 001, Karnataka, India.

***Corresponding author:**

[*4]Dr. Srinivasulu M. V, Associate Professor, Department of Botany, Govt. Science College, Nrupathunga University, Bengaluru – 560 001, Karnataka, India.

Email: keshava.micro@gmail.com

Abstract:

Carbon sequestration, the process by which carbon dioxide is captured from the atmosphere and stored in natural reservoirs, has emerged as a critical strategy in mitigating climate change. While technological solutions garner significant attention, the capacity of terrestrial, aquatic, and marine ecosystems to sequester carbon remains underexplored. This chapter explores the diverse mechanisms through which ecosystems capture and store carbon, highlighting their immense potential as nature-based solutions to climate change. Terrestrial ecosystems, including forests, grasslands, and wetlands, play a pivotal role in carbon sequestration. Aquatic ecosystems, encompassing freshwater bodies like lakes, rivers, and wetlands, as well as coastal habitats like mangroves, salt marshes, and seagrasses, exhibit remarkable carbon sequestration potential. Coastal ecosystems, with their high productivity and extensive root systems, sequester carbon in soils and organic matter, serving as crucial blue carbon reservoirs. Marine ecosystems, including the vast expanses of the open ocean and the rich biodiversity of coral reefs, also contribute significantly to carbon sequestration. Phytoplankton in the ocean's surface waters play a key role in the biological pump, transporting carbon from the surface to the deep ocean through sinking particles. Coral reefs, renowned for their biodiversity and ecosystem services, store carbon in their calcium carbonate skeletons and organic matter. Harnessing nature's potential in carbon sequestration requires holistic conservation and restoration approaches that prioritize ecosystem health and resilience. Protecting and restoring forests, wetlands, and coastal habitats, as well as implementing sustainable land and ocean management practices, are crucial steps in enhancing carbon sequestration capacities. Terrestrial, aquatic, and marine ecosystems represent invaluable allies in the fight against climate change. Unlocking their full potential in carbon sequestration requires concerted efforts to preserve and restore natural habitats, alongside ambitious climate action at local, national, and global scales. By embracing nature-based solutions, we can harness the power of ecosystems to safeguard the planet's climate and biodiversity for future generations

Keywords: Carbon sequestration; ecosystem; Climate change mitigation; Phytoplankton; Biological pump; Ecosystem resilience.

1. Introduction:

Terrestrial Marvels: Forests, Grasslands, and Soils: Forest ecosystems account for the majority of ice-free land surface among all terrestrial ecosystems. The greatest stock or absolute quantity of the live forest biomass is found in trees, which are the primary structural element of forest ecosystems. Approximately 677 petagrams (Pg) of biomass are found in forests worldwide, with trees accounting for 80% of all biomass. Through photosynthesis, forest ecosystems take in significant amounts of CO_2 from the atmosphere and release a significant portion of the fixed carbon back into the atmosphere through auto- and heterotrophic respiration. Nonetheless, soil, trash, and biomass both above and below ground hold a tiny amount of absorbed carbon. Forests contain almost half of the terrestrial carbon sink (Lorenz and Lal, 2010).

Mechanism of Carbon Sequestration of Forests: The process of removing atmospheric carbon dioxide and storing it for a long time in order to prevent hazardous climate change effects and slow down global warming is known as carbon sequestration. Put differently, it encompasses the act of extracting carbon from the atmosphere and storing it in a reservoir. Carbon pools are another name for these carbon reservoirs or storages. A system or mechanism with the ability to accumulate or release carbon is referred to as a carbon pool. It could be caused by humans or by nature. Soils, wood products, forests, and the atmosphere are a few examples. Minerals and a complex mixture of both living and dead organic materials make up a forest's carbon pools. Carbon dioxide is stored in geological formations called "human-induced carbon pools." The term "carbon stock" refers to the amount of carbon in a pool; any modification can be described as a "stock exchange" (Dhanwantri et al., 2014).

Around 2100 Gt of carbon are found worldwide in terrestrial ecosystems, with soils storing more than two third of this amount. While a sizable inert carbon pool may become active when exposed to novel environmental conditions, a portion of this soil carbon pool is quite changeable in both space and time. Soils may transform from being sinks of atmospheric carbon to being generators of it due to rapid climatic changes. Given their great capacity to store carbon, soils may have a role in reducing the amount of CO^2 in the atmosphere. However, it is still unclear how soil carbon sequestration is regulated, and it is also uncertain how to extrapolate findings from short-term empirical investigations to long-term estimates of global carbon balances (Deyn et al., 2008).

2. Role of Healthy Soils and their Microbial Communities in Storing Carbon:

Millions of microorganisms that are important for crop productivity and improved soil fertility are found in soil. The preservation of fundamental soil processes related to nutrient availability, agricultural yields, and literal decomposition depends on soil microorganisms. The quantity and quality of soil organic matter, pH, biomass density, and redox potential limitations all affect the physicochemical characteristics of soil. The dynamics, composition, and soil structure of the microscopic culture are all significantly impacted by these (Shah et al., 2021).

Sequestering carbon (C) in soil involves moving and safely storing atmospheric CO_2 into the soil's organic carbon (SOC) pool, which is composed of recalcitrant humus and biochar, and the soil's inorganic carbon (SIC) pool, which is composed of secondary carbonates. Its significance stems from the need to counteract the rise in atmospheric CO_2 enrichment from 280 parts per million in 1750 to 381 parts per million in 2007, as well as its advantages for soil quality and agronomic production. The estimated soil C sink capacity, resulting from past land use and soil degradation, is 78±12 Pg, or 10-60 Mg/ha. The two main methods of sequestering SOC are:

(i)   Restoring degraded or desertified soils by converting them to a perennial land use; and

(ii)   using advised management techniques such agroforestry, manuring, no-till farming, and adding biochar as a soil amendment (Lal, 2008).

3. The Impact of Deforestation and Land-Use Changes on Terrestrial Carbon Sequestration Potential:

Changes in land use have an impact on soil and vegetation carbon stocks as well as greenhouse gas emissions. The amount of carbon stored in soil and vegetation varies depending on the type of land use, as does the potential rate at which the carbon stock changes. Soil organic carbon (SOC) stores beneath agriculture are typically lower than those beneath grassland or forests. SOC stocks in forests are often higher than those in pastures. It has been discovered that whereas conversions from forest to farmland, pasture, or cropland to pasture reduce SOC levels, conversions from pasture to cropland typically enhance SOC stocks. In addition to storing carbon in the soil, forests also store a significant quantity of carbon in biomass (Schulp, et al., 2008).

4. Aquatic Wonders: Wetlands, Seagrasses, and Algae:

While increasing CO_2 levels in freshwater and marine environments encourage photosynthesis and increase competition from algae and higher plants like seagrasses, lower pH levels brought on by increased CO_2 dissolution can be detrimental to fish, sea urchins, and most importantly, organisms with shells like corals, mollusks, pteropods, and coccolithophores. It may seem counterintuitive, but rising CO_2 directly endangers calcifying (shell-forming) species by lowering carbonate concentrations in surface water. Carbonate concentrations must be higher above saturation thresholds in order to generate carbonate-based shells. Greater CO_2 dissolution causes the pH to decrease with atmospheric CO_2 concentration, from pre-industrial values of approximately 8.2 to approximately 7.9 in 2100. The equilibrium shifts significantly from carbonate to bicarbonate as a result of these small pH decreases, which happen close to the pKa between bicarbonate and carbonate. While carbonate levels fall below the saturation point for the creation of calcium carbonate shells, cooler, high-latitude water crosses the threshold sooner. Higher bicarbonate concentrations in seawater stimulate algae photosynthesis (Sage, 2019).

5. Role of Seagrasses in Coastal Carbon Capture and Storage:

A quarter of the productivity of seagrass meadows is exported on average, and some of it may travel hundreds or thousands of kilometers and aid in the storage of carbon in the deep oceans. A increasing amount of research indicates that there is a chance for carbon to move from seagrass to inshore habitats, especially mangroves, at least in certain locations and under certain circumstances (Huxham, et al., 2018).

It is predicted that in near-shore environments, coral-dominated communities may give way to algae- and seagrass-dominated communities in a high CO_2 world. This is because algae and seagrasses compete with corals and other shelled organisms, and subtle fitness reductions caused by pH and carbonate declines are magnified in mixed communities. Known as "the other CO_2 problem," ocean acidification is thought to have contributed to the extinction of some species during previous mass extinctions (Sage, 2019).

6. The Contribution of Algae and Phytoplankton in Marine Environments, Emphasizing their Importance in Carbon Sequestration:

Microalgae are quickly expanding organisms that can absorb large amounts of CO_2 and create a variety of biomass. Higher plants are not as effective at fixing CO_2 as microalgae are. Typical sources of CO_2 are

    (i)   Carbon dioxide in the atmosphere;

    (ii)   Flue gas and other industrial exhaust gases; and

    (iii)   Soluble carbonates such $NaHCO_3$ and $Na2CO_3$.

The relationship between microalgae efficiency and CO_2 concentration in the growing atmosphere is strong; the higher the CO_2 concentration, the better the growth and, ultimately, the higher productivity. The effectiveness and cost-competitiveness of the CO_2 biomitigation process are greatly impacted by the choice of appropriate microalgae strains. High growth and CO_2 consumption rates, as well as a high tolerance to CO_2 concentrations and trace elements of exhaust gases like SOx and NOx (nitrogen oxides), to be more precise, are desirable characteristics for high CO_2 fixation (NO and NO_2). There are differences in the maximal CO_2 tolerance capability of different microalgae. The supply of CO_2 helps to regulate the culture's pH. Since CO_2 lowers a solution's pH, species that thrive in acidic environments are typically more tolerant of high CO_2 concentrations (Singh and Ahluwalia, 2013).

7. Marine Miracles: Coral Reefs and Deep-Sea Ecosystems:

One of the most vulnerable and productive marine ecosystems is the coral reef. The long-running CO_2 "source-sink" controversy over coral reefs has intensified due to the global reduction of coral reefs brought on by climate change and human activity. This decline has already impacted the processes of coral calcification and carbon cycling in the reef ecosystem. Given the intricate biogeochemical processes in the reef ecosystem and the distinct mixotrophic lifestyle of the reef-building corals, coral reefs are an important carbon sink even though coral calcification is accompanied by the release of CO_2 into the atmosphere. The study reduces confusion surrounding the coral reef CO_2 "source-sink" debate, investigate potential ecological regulations and pathways to convert coral reefs from carbon sources to sinks, and provide theoretical framework and technical support for the deployment of ocean negative carbon emissions and the national carbon neutrality strategy. All of these efforts are undertaken with the goal of increasing coral resilience to climate change (Shi et al., 2021).

Huge carbonate synthesis by the organisms is a characteristic of coral reefs. It is well known that photosynthesis, which is regulated by the carbonate equilibrium in saltwater, is connected to fast calcification. These simultaneous impacts on calcification and photosynthetic enhancement are anticipated to manifest in a reef ecosystem that is cut off from the outer ocean during low tide, in addition to the internal pool of organisms. Measurements conducted on the fringing type Shiraho Reef in the Ryukyu Islands revealed a noticeable daily variation in the water's pH, total alkalinity, total carbon dioxide content, and degree of carbonate saturation. This setting provides the right conditions for these coexisting effects to manifest. During daytime and night time slack-water phases, respectively, the photosynthetic augmentation of calcification and the respiratory encouragement of decalcification were detected. These combined effects seem to be crucial for fluorishing coral reef populations, particularly the photosynthetic improvement of calcification (Suzuki et al., 1995).

8. The Contribution of Deep-Sea Ecosystems, such as Hydrothermal Vents and Cold Seeps, in Sequestering Carbon Over Long Periods:
Although the deep ocean and seafloor are thought to be huge, dark, isolated, and uninhabitable, they actually play a vital role in human existence due to the services they offer. Though our knowledge of the deep sea's operations is still limited, a variety of supporting, supplying, regulating, and cultural services become clear when viewed in a synoptically manner. The biological pump lessens the effect of anthropogenic carbon emission by moving carbon from the atmosphere into deep-ocean water masses that are separated over extended periods of time. Methane oxidation by micro-organisms traps carbon in authigenic carbonates and prevents the release of another powerful greenhouse gas into the atmosphere. All faunal size classes regenerate nutrients, which supply the components needed to support fisheries and surface productivity. Microbial processes also detoxify a variety of chemicals.

Fish stocks, vast bio prospecting potential, and elements and energy deposits that are presently being mined and will become more significant in the near future are just a few of the many resources found in the deep sea. The fascination and enigma, the unusual organisms, and the vast unknown, which have served as a source of creativity and inspiration since almost the dawn of civilization, are all beneficial to society. The resulting services are only useful after centuries of coordinated activity, even though numerous processes take place on timescales ranging from years to microns. This enormous, gloomy ecosystem, which encompasses much of the world, has activities that directly affect humans in a number of ways; however, the same characteristics that set it apart from terrestrial (Thurber et al., 2014).

9. The Threats Posed by Climate Change and Human Activities to Marine Biodiversity and its Impact on Carbon Sequestration:

The effects of climate change are multiplying for all environmental issues. Climate change is the biggest threat to coastal ecosystems globally, but humans have been negatively affecting coastal areas locally for ages. Many coastal ecosystems are exposed to excess nutrients, heavy metals, and other land-derived contaminants (like sediments and microplastics). Additionally, many coastal areas have been reclaimed from the sea for groundwater extraction (which causes saltwater intrusion), industrial expansion, cultivation, aquaculture, firewood, and food production. The deterioration or extinction of coastal ecosystems can be attributed to a number of regional human influences, many of which are still becoming worse overall. Climate change and regional human activities are making coastal areas more susceptible to interactions. Scientists are well-versed in the interactions between algae and ocean waters, including warming and nutrient deposition (Muruganandam et al., 2023).

Rebuilding teleost fish populations to high abundance is another benefit of marine reserves, as these species are important players in the marine inorganic carbon cycle. For osmoregulation, teleost fish consume seawater. In their alkaline intestine, they precipitate nearly all of the calcium and some of the magnesium they intake into carbonate minerals, which they then expel from their stomach as high-magnesium calcite crystals. Compared to the calcite and aragonite produced by marine calcifiers such coccolithophores, foraminifera, and corals, these fish carbonates dissolve at shallower depths.

$$CaCO_3 + CO_2 + H_2O \Leftrightarrow 2HCO_3^{-}{}^{+Ca^{2+}}$$

Compared to calcite or aragonite, the near-surface dissolution of fish carbonates increases alkalinity and has a quicker effect on surface pH and seawater buffering. The build-up of high-magnesium calcite in shelf sediments may serve as an initial buffer against acidification's decreased saturation state (Roberts et al., 2017).

10. Conservation Strategies and Sustainable Practices:

The range of various living forms on Earth, comprising various plants, animals, and microorganisms, along with the genes they carry and the ecosystems they create, is known as biodiversity. Within a region, biome, or planet, it relates to genetic variety, ecosystem variation, and species variation (number of species). In light of the variety of habitats, biotic communities, and ecological processes found in the biosphere, biodiversity is essential for a number of reasons, such as enhancing the aesthetic value of the natural world and advancing our material well-being by supplying resources like food, fuel, wood, medicine, and fodder. The foundation of life is biodiversity. It provides the food, drink, and oxygen that organisms need to survive.

It provides the food, drink, and oxygen that organisms need to survive. Wetlands filter pollutants from water, plants and trees absorb carbon dioxide to slow down global warming, and fungi and bacteria decompose organic matter to fertilize the soil. Empirical research has demonstrated a connection between the richness of native species and both ecological health and human well-being. The maintenance of the ecosystem services provided by biodiversity is achieved by a variety of processes, including soil formation and protection, water conservation and purification, hydrological cycle maintenance, biochemical cycle regulation, absorption and breakdown of pollutants and waste materials through decomposition, and determination and regulation of the global climate (Rawatand Agarwal, 2015).

11. International Efforts for Biodiversity Conservation:

In an effort to increase global commitment and involvement in biodiversity conservation, a number of international treaties and accords have been established. Among these are:

- Rio–de-Janeiro under the United Nations Conference on Environment and Development (UNCED)/ Earth Summit African Convention on Conservation of nature and natural resources.
- The Ramsar Convention on Wetlands of international importance.
- International Union for the Conservation of nature (World Conservation Union).
- Convention on International trade for endangered species (CITES).
- International Convention for the Protection on birds.
- International Board for Plant genetic resources.
- World Resources Institute.
- World Wide Fund for Nature.
- Convention on Conservation of migratory species of wild animals.

- International Convention for the Regulation of whaling.
- UNESCO programme on Man and biosphere.

12. Indian Efforts for Biodiversity Conservation:

In India, preserving and advancing biodiversity has always been essential to civilization and culture. The thousands of sacred groves spread around the nation serve as evidence of this. The biodiversity of plants and animals is essential to the traditional Indian agricultural and medical systems. India was among the first countries to ratify the Convention on Biological Diversity (CBD) of the United Nations. India has always had legal provisions addressing biodiversity-related issues long before CBD. The management of forests and the preservation of forest land are covered by the Indian Forest Act of 1927 and the Forest (Conservation) Act of 1980, respectively (Rawat and Agarwal, 2015).

The Wildlife (Protection) Act of 1972 was created to safeguard wild animals, birds, and plants. Its main objectives are to preserve, propagate, or enhance wildlife and its habitat by creating national parks, sanctuaries, and other similar establishments. Furthermore, a section of the Act forbids the picking and uprooting of some plants. India has more than 600 Protected Areas, which make up 5% of the nation's total geographic area and are connected by a network of National Parks, Wildlife Sanctuaries, and Conservation Reserves, despite the pressure of population growth on the land. India offers specific programs for a few well-known endangered species, such as elephants and tigers. The country-level tiger status assessment conducted in 2010 revealed that the estimated number of tigers had increased from 1411 in 2006 to 1706 in 2010 (Rawat and Agarwal, 2015).

13. Sustainable Practices and Policies that Promote Carbon Sequestration:

The benefits that humans receive from the ecosystem carbon sequestration process, which is essential for stabilizing the natural basis for development, controlling climate change, and assisting in the fulfillment of the Sustainable Development Goals (SDGs), is known as the ecosystem carbon sequestration service (ECSS). We still need to figure out how ECSS fits into the SDGs, though. Here, we determined the contribution of ECSS to the SDGs using regression analysis, downscaling localization SDG indicators, and mechanism analysis, using the Loess Plateau (LP) region of China as an example (Yin et al., 2023).

The post-industrial age is characterized by the awareness of forests' broader range of benefits. Multi-functional forestry (MFF) is characterized by a change in focus from commodity to non-commodity outputs, or from maximizing the production of material items (like wood) to more general goals of offering a variety of ecosystem services (ESS). The advantages that people derive from ecosystems are known as ESS. According to the Millennium Ecosystem Assessment (MEA, 2005), humans are essential components of ecosystems and engage in dynamic interactions with other ecosystem components. Moreover, changes in human behavior are directly and indirectly responsible for environmental changes. The MEA classifies the ESS into supporting, provisioning, regulatory, cultural, and social sectors in light of cross-scale concerns, social, economic, and environmental linkages, and multiple outcomes of natural resource usage (Nijnik and Miller, 2013).

- Every other ESS's production depends on and requires supporting services. These consist of soil formation, carbon and water storage, fertility, photosynthesis, primary production, biodiversity, nutrient and water cycle, and soil formation.
- Provisioning services: genetic, biochemical, natural pharmaceutical and medical resources; fresh water; food; fuel; fiber/wood; and ornamental resources.
- The benefits that come from controlling ecological processes, such as those related to pollination, disease and insect control, air quality, climate, water, and erosion control, water purification, and natural hazard control, are known as regulating services.

The non-material benefits that people receive from ecosystems through spiritual enrichment, cognitive growth, introspection, leisure, and aesthetic experiences are referred to as cultural and social services. These benefits take into account the values of the landscape as well as the diversity of cultures and ethnologies (Nijnik,and Miller, 2013).

14. Future Directions: Enhancing Carbon Sequestration Capacities:

Carbon capture and sequestration (CCS) is now possible thanks to new invention and technology; however it requires large upfront expenditures and is similar to waste management. As a result, CCSU biotechnology has drawn increased attention in an effort to develop value chains that reduce expenses. However, due to financial limits, human capacity issues, and the requirement to adapt large-scale industrial equipment with new installations, CCSU's existing state-of-the-art is inadequate. The CCSU capacity now in existence will not be sufficient to address the climate catastrophe at the present rate of CO_2 emission (Schweitzer*et al.*, 2021). Many industrial companies, industry collaboratives, and government organizations use road-mapping methodologies in their planning processes. There are many different kinds of road maps, and the phrase "road mapping" has been used to refer to a wide range of activities. Road maps for emerging technologies provide a structure for overseeing and monitoring the intricate, dynamic RandD process required to accomplish significant strategic objectives. These road maps provide a visual representation of how certain RandD projects might produce the combined technical capabilities required to meet strategic goals.

The carbon processing technology platform is the first one. This platform's main goal is to develop cutting-edge chemical technologies, which may then be used to produce technologies with ancillary advantages and platforms for capture and separation. The potential success of geological and ocean sequestration solutions will also depend on how well capture and separation technologies isolate relatively pure CO_2 for transportation and storage. The following technological platforms will be needed:

- Chemical and physical absorption, including the creation of new absorbents.
- Chemical and physical adsorption.
- Mineralization/bio-mineralization, including the creation of better reaction pathways for the formation of carbonates and bicarbonates for geologic and oceanic dissolution and sequestration.
- Low-temperature distillation systems.
- Novel concepts, including improved techniques for generating CO_2 clathrates and the use of algal bio-scrubbers on emissions streams.

References:

1. Lorenz, K. and Lal, R. (2010). Introduction. In: Carbon Sequestration in Forest Ecosystems. Springer, Dordrecht. https://doi.org/10.1007/978-90-481-3266-9_1.
2. Dhanwantri, K., Sharma, P., Mehta, S., and Prakash, P. (2014). Carbon sequestration, its methods and significance. *Environmental sustainability: Concepts, Principles, Evidences and Innovations,151(2), 151-157.*
3. De Deyn, G.B., Cornelissen, J.H., and Bardgett, R.D. (2008). Plant functional traits and soil carbon sequestration in contrasting biomes. *Ecology letters, 11(5),* 516-531. doi: 10.1111/j.1461-0248.2008.01164.x.
4. Shah, K. K., Tripathi, S., Tiwari, I., Shrestha, J., Modi,B., Paudel, N., and Das, B. D. (2021). Role of soil microbes in sustainable crop production and soil health: A review. *Agricultural Science and Technology, 13(2),* 109-118.
5. Lal, R. (2008). Carbon sequerstration in soil. *CABI Reviews,* (2008), 20-pp. https://doi.org/10.1079/PAVSNNR20083030.

6. Schulp, C. J., Nabuurs, G. J., and Verburg, P. H. (2008). Future carbon sequestration in Europe—Effects of land use change. *Agriculture, Ecosystems and Environment, 127(3-4),* 251-264. https://doi.org/10.1016/j.agee.2008.04.010.

7. Sage, R. F. (2020). Global change biology: a primer. *Global Change Biology,26(1),* 3-30. https://doi.org/10.1111/gcb.14893.

8. Huxham, M., Whitlock, D., Githaiga, M., and Dencer-Brown, A. (2018). Carbon in the coastal seascape: how interactions between mangrove forests, seagrass meadows and tidal marshes influence carbon storage. *Current Forestry Reports, 4,* 101–110 https://doi.org/10.1007/s40725-018-0077-4.

9. Singh, U.B., and Ahluwalia, A. S. (2013). Microalgae: a promising tool for carbon sequestration. *Mitigation and Adaptation Strategies for Global Change, 18(1),*73-95.

10. Shi, T., Zheng, X., Zhang, H., Wang, Q., and Zhong, X. (2021). Coral reefs: potential blue carbon sinks for climate mitigation. *Bulletin of Chinese Academy of Sciences (Chinese Version), 36(3),* 270-278. DOI: https://doi.org/10.16418/j.issn.1000-3045.20210217102.

11. Suzuki, A., Nakamori, T. and Kayanne, H. (1995). The mechanism of production enhancement in coral reef carbonate systems: model and empirical results. *Sedimentary Geology, 99(3-4),* 259-280. ISSN 0037-0738. https://doi.org/10.1016/0037-0738(95)00048-D.

12. Thurber, A. R., Sweetman, A. K., Narayanaswamy, B. E., Jones, D. O. B., Ingels, J., and Hansman, R. L. (2014). Ecosystem function and services provided by the deep sea. *Biogeosciences, 11,* 3941–3963. https://doi.org/10.5194/bg-11-3941-2014.

13. Priya A. K, Muruganandam M, SivarethinamohanRajamanickam, Sujatha Sivarethinamohan, Madhava Krishna Reddy Gaddam, PriyaVelusamy, Gomathi R, GokulanRavindiran, Thirumala Rao Gurugubelli, Senthil Kumar Muniasamy. (2023). Impact of climate change and anthropogenic activities on aquatic ecosystem – A review. *Environmental Research, 238(2),* 117233. ISSN 0013-9351. https://doi.org/10.1016/j.envres.2023.117233.

14. Roberts, C. M., O'Leary, B. C., McCauley, D. J., Cury, P. M., Duarte, C. M., Lubchenco, J., … andCastilla, J. C. (2017). Marine reserves can mitigate and promote adaptation to climate change. *Proceedings of the National Academy of Sciences, 114(24),* 6167-6175.

15. Rawat, U., and Agarwal, N. (2015). Biodiversity: Concept, threats and conservation. *Environment Conservation Journal, 16*(3), 19–28. https://doi.org/10.36953/ECJ.2015.16303.

16. Caichun Yin, Wenwu Zhao, Jingqiao Ye, Monica Muroki, Paulo Pereira. (2023). Ecosystem carbon sequestration service supports the Sustainable Development Goals progress. *Journal of Environmental Management.* Volume *330*, 117155. ISSN 0301-4797. https://doi.org/10.1016/j.jenvman.2022.117155.

17. Maria Nijnik, David Miller. Targeting Sustainable Provision of Forest Ecosystem Services with Special Focus on Carbon Sequestration, Editor(s): R. Matyssek, N. Clarke, P. Cudlin, T.N. Mikkelsen, J.-P. Tuovinen, G. Wieser, and E. Paoletti. (2013). Developments in Environmental Science. Elsevier, Volume 13, 547-568. ISSN 1474-8177. https://doi.org/10.1016/B978-0-08-098349-3.00025-6.

18. Schweitzer, H., Aalto, N. J., Busch, W., Chan, D. T. C., Chiesa, M., Elvevoll, E. O., ... & Bernstein, H. C. (2021). Innovating carbon-capture biotechnologies through ecosystem-inspired solutions. *One Earth, 4*(1), 49-59.

19. Reichle, D., Houghton, J., Kane, B., and Ekmann, J. (1999). *Carbon sequestration research and development* (No. DOE/SC/FE-1). Oak Ridge National Lab. (ORNL), Oak Ridge, TN (United States); National Energy Technology Lab., Pittsburgh, PA (US); National Energy Technology Lab., Morgantown, WV (US).

2. Role of Education in Fostering Sustainable Development

Dr. Neelima Sachwani

Assistant Professor, Gautam Buddha University, Greater Noida, U.P

Email: rsneelimasachwani@gmail.com

Abstract:

Education is a critical tool in achieving sustainable development, equipping individuals with the knowledge, skills, and values necessary to address global challenges such as climate change, biodiversity loss, and social inequity. This article explores the multifaceted role of education in promoting sustainability, highlights innovative educational approaches, and examines case studies that demonstrate successful integration of sustainability into educational frameworks. By fostering critical thinking and empowering individuals, education can drive sustainable practices and contribute to a resilient and equitable future.

Keywords: Sustainable development, education, sustainability, environmental education, critical thinking, equity.

1. Introduction:

Sustainable development, as defined by the Brundtland Report (1987), aims to meet the needs of the present without compromising the ability of future generations to meet their own needs. This definition underscores the importance of balancing environmental, economic, and social dimensions to ensure long-term viability and equity. As global challenges such as climate change, biodiversity loss, and social inequity intensify, the role of education in fostering sustainable development has become increasingly critical. Education is universally acknowledged as a fundamental element in achieving sustainable development. It provides the foundation for improving quality of life, promoting social cohesion, and fostering economic growth while ensuring environmental protection (UNESCO, 2014). Education for Sustainable Development (ESD) aims to equip individuals with the knowledge, skills, values, and attitudes necessary to become active participants in sustainable development efforts. The concept of ESD has evolved significantly over the past few decades, driven by global initiatives and policy frameworks. The Tbilisi Declaration (1977) was one of the earliest international agreements to highlight the importance of environmental education, setting the stage for subsequent developments. Agenda 21, adopted at the United Nations Conference on Environment and Development (UNCED) in 1992, further emphasized the need for educational reforms to address environmental and developmental challenges (UN, 1992). These initiatives have paved the way for the integration of sustainability into educational systems worldwide.

- The United Nations Decade of Education for Sustainable Development (2005-2014) marked a significant milestone in advancing ESD. It sought to integrate the principles, values, and practices of sustainable development into all aspects of education and learning (UNESCO, 2014). The Global Action Programme on ESD, launched in 2015, continues to build on this momentum, aiming to generate and scale up action in all levels and areas of education and learning (UNESCO, 2017). The importance of ESD is reflected in its inclusion in the United Nations Sustainable Development Goals (SDGs), particularly Goal 4, which aims to ensure inclusive and equitable quality education and promote lifelong learning opportunities for all. Target 4.7 specifically calls for all learners to acquire the knowledge and skills needed to promote sustainable development, including education for sustainable development and sustainable lifestyles, human rights, gender equality, and global citizenship (UN, 2015). Research indicates that ESD has a profound impact on student outcomes. It enhances environmental awareness, critical thinking skills, and civic engagement, preparing students to address complex sustainability challenges (Sterling, 2010). By fostering a holistic understanding of sustainability, ESD encourages individuals to adopt sustainable lifestyles and engage in responsible decision-making processes.

- Education for Sustainable Development (ESD) emphasizes a holistic approach to learning that integrates various disciplines to provide a comprehensive understanding of sustainability. This approach recognizes that environmental, economic, and social dimensions of sustainability are interconnected and must be addressed collectively (UNESCO, 2017).

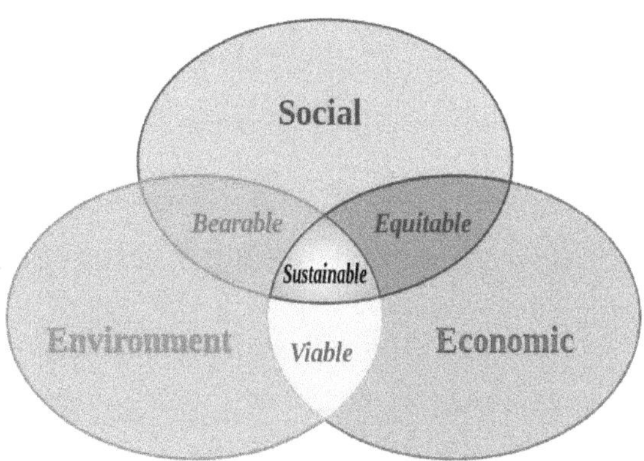

Figure 1: Interconnected Dimensions of Sustainable Development

(https://upload.wikimedia.org/wikipedia/commons/7/70/Sustainable_development.svg)

In this figure, education serves as a vital bridge connecting the three dimensions environmental, social, and economic aspects of sustainable development, fostering an integrated perspective that enables learners to understand and address complex sustainability challenges. Education empowers individuals with the knowledge, skills, and values needed to promote environmental stewardship, social equity, and sustainable economic practices, thereby contributing to a more sustainable future for all. Education for Sustainable Development (ESD) emphasizes holistic, interdisciplinary approaches that integrate sustainability into curricula at all levels of education. ESD fosters critical thinking, problem-solving, and participatory learning, empowering individuals to make informed decisions and take responsible actions for environmental integrity, economic viability, and a just society (Tilbury, 2011). Despite its recognized importance, the implementation of ESD faces several challenges. These include inadequate teacher training, insufficient resources, and resistance to curricular changes. Addressing these barriers requires concerted efforts from policymakers, educational institutions, and communities to create supportive environments for ESD (Barth et al., 2007). This article explores the multifaceted role of education in promoting sustainable development, highlighting innovative educational approaches and examining case studies that demonstrate successful integration of sustainability into educational frameworks. By fostering critical thinking and empowering individuals, education can drive sustainable practices and contribute to a resilient and equitable future.

2. Literature Review:

The role of education in sustainable development has been extensively studied, revealing its significant impact on fostering environmental awareness, critical thinking, and civic engagement. Historically, the concept of Education for Sustainable Development (ESD) has evolved through global initiatives such as the Tbilisi Declaration (1977) and Agenda 21 (1992). The Tbilisi Declaration was one of the earliest international agreements to highlight the importance of environmental education, setting the foundation for subsequent educational reforms aimed at addressing environmental and developmental challenges (UNESCO, 1977).

- The adoption of Agenda 21 at the United Nations Conference on Environment and Development (UNCED) in 1992 further emphasized the need for integrating sustainability into educational systems worldwide (UN, 1992). This agenda called for the reorientation of education towards sustainable development, emphasizing interdisciplinary learning, critical thinking, and problem-solving skills necessary for addressing complex sustainability issues. Research indicates that ESD significantly enhances students' understanding of sustainability and their ability to engage in sustainable practices. Sterling (2010) argues that ESD fosters transformative learning, which fundamentally changes the way individuals perceive and interact with the world. This transformative learning process encourages critical reflection and promotes a deeper understanding of sustainability issues, leading to more informed and responsible actions.

- Biasutti and Frate (2017) conducted a study that demonstrated the positive impact of ESD on students' attitudes and behaviours towards sustainability. The study found that students exposed to ESD programs exhibited higher levels of pro-environmental behaviour and sustainability literacy. These findings highlight the importance of incorporating ESD into educational curricula to cultivate environmentally responsible citizens. Despite its benefits, the implementation of ESD faces several challenges. Barth et al. (2007) identify key barriers such as inadequate teacher training, insufficient resources, and resistance to curricular changes. Effective ESD requires well-trained educators who can integrate sustainability concepts into various subjects and foster a learning environment that encourages critical thinking and active participation. Professional development and support networks for teachers are crucial for overcoming these challenges and ensuring the successful implementation of ESD.

- The United Nations Decade of Education for Sustainable Development (2005-2014) marked a significant milestone in advancing ESD. This global initiative aimed to integrate the principles, values, and practices of sustainable development into all aspects of education and learning (UNESCO, 2014). The decade's efforts culminated in the launch of the Global Action Programme on ESD in 2015, which seeks to generate and scale up action in all levels and areas of education and learning (UNESCO, 2017). Case studies provide valuable insights into successful ESD implementations. For instance, the Green School in Bali, Indonesia, is renowned for its innovative approach to integrating sustainability into its core curriculum. This school emphasizes experiential learning and community engagement, resulting in significant environmental stewardship and sustainability awareness among its students (Green School Bali, 2020). Furthermore, surveys conducted across multiple schools in Europe reveal that students participating in ESD programs are more likely to engage in sustainable practices such as recycling, energy conservation, and community service (de Haan, 2006). These findings underscore the transformative potential of ESD in fostering sustainable behaviours and practices at both individual and community levels.

3. Methodology:

This research employs a mixed-methods approach, combining quantitative surveys and qualitative case studies to examine the role of education in promoting sustainable development. Data were collected from various educational institutions implementing ESD programs and analysed to assess their impact on student behaviour and community sustainability initiatives.

4. Findings and Discussions:

The analysis of the role of education in sustainable development reveals several key findings that highlight the transformative potential of Education for Sustainable Development (ESD). This section discusses these findings in detail, supported by evidence from relevant studies and case examples.

One of the primary findings is that ESD significantly enhances sustainability literacy and awareness among students. Biasutti and Frate (2017) conducted a study that demonstrated the effectiveness of ESD in improving students' understanding of sustainability concepts and principles. Students who participated in ESD programs exhibited higher levels of sustainability literacy, which includes knowledge of environmental issues, awareness of the interconnectedness of ecological, social, and economic systems, and the ability to critically assess sustainability-related information.

Another significant finding is that ESD promotes pro-environmental behaviours among students. Studies have shown that students exposed to ESD are more likely to engage in sustainable practices such as recycling, energy conservation, and participation in community environmental initiatives. For example, de Haan (2006) found that students who participated in ESD programs in European schools were more inclined to adopt sustainable lifestyles and contribute to their communities' environmental efforts. This behaviour change is attributed to the experiential and transformative learning approaches employed in ESD. By engaging students in hands-on activities, critical reflection, and community projects, ESD fosters a sense of environmental stewardship and responsibility. The case of the Green School in Bali, Indonesia, further illustrates this point. The school's curriculum, which emphasizes experiential learning and community engagement, has led to significant environmental stewardship and sustainability awareness among its students (Green School Bali, 2020).

Despite its benefits, the implementation of ESD faces several challenges. One of the main barriers is the lack of adequately trained educators. Teachers often lack the necessary skills and knowledge to effectively integrate sustainability into their teaching practices. Barth et al., (2007) highlight the importance of professional development programs in equipping teachers with the competencies required for ESD. These programs should focus on interdisciplinary teaching, critical thinking, and experiential learning methodologies. Another challenge is the insufficient allocation of resources for ESD. Schools and educational institutions often struggle with limited funding and support for sustainability initiatives. Addressing this issue requires concerted efforts from policymakers, educational authorities, and the broader community to prioritize and invest in ESD.

Global policy frameworks and initiatives play a crucial role in advancing ESD. The United Nations Decade of Education for Sustainable Development (2005-2014) and the subsequent Global Action Programme on ESD have provided significant impetus for integrating sustainability into educational systems worldwide (UNESCO, 2014; UNESCO, 2017). These initiatives have raised awareness, mobilized resources, and fostered international collaboration to promote ESD. The inclusion of ESD in the United Nations Sustainable Development Goals (SDGs), particularly Goal 4.7, underscores the global commitment to education as a means to achieve sustainable development (UN, 2015). This goal calls for ensuring that all learners acquire the knowledge and skills needed to promote sustainable development, including through education for sustainable development, sustainable lifestyles, human rights, gender equality, and global citizenship. Innovative educational models and practices are essential for the successful implementation of ESD. Schools like the Green School in Bali and various programs in Europe exemplify how innovative approaches to education can foster sustainability. These models emphasize experiential learning, interdisciplinary teaching, and strong community involvement, creating a dynamic and engaging learning environment that promotes sustainability (Green School Bali, 2020; de Haan, 2006). Moreover, the development of key competencies for sustainability, as proposed by Wiek et al., (2011), provides a framework for designing effective ESD programs. These competencies include systems-thinking, anticipatory, normative, strategic, and interpersonal competencies, all of which are crucial for addressing complex sustainability challenges.

5. Conclusion:

Education plays a pivotal role in achieving sustainable development by fostering a generation with the knowledge, skills, and attitudes necessary to tackle global challenges such as climate change, social inequality, and biodiversity loss. While challenges remain, innovative educational approaches and strong institutional support can enhance the effectiveness of ESD. Continued research and investment in education are essential for driving sustainable practices and ensuring a resilient future. This role of education is increasingly recognized and integrated into global policy frameworks, emphasizing its significance in fostering a sustainable future. The evolving landscape of Education for Sustainable Development (ESD) highlights its transformative potential. The integration of holistic and interdisciplinary approaches in ESD encourages learners to view sustainability issues through a multifaceted lens, promoting a deeper understanding of the interconnectedness between environmental, social, and economic dimensions. This comprehensive perspective is essential for developing the critical thinking and problem-solving skills required to address complex sustainability challenges. Transformative learning, a key component of ESD, plays a crucial role in reshaping individuals' perceptions and actions towards sustainability. By fostering critical reflection and experiential learning, ESD helps individuals question their assumptions and adopt more sustainable lifestyles. This process of transformation is fundamental to creating a culture of sustainability that permeates all aspects of society.

Despite its recognized importance, the implementation of ESD faces significant challenges. These include inadequate teacher training, limited resources, and resistance to curricular changes. Addressing these barriers requires comprehensive support from policymakers, educational institutions, and communities to create an enabling environment for ESD. Professional development programs and support networks for educators are particularly critical in enhancing their capacity to deliver effective ESD. The success of ESD can be seen in various innovative educational models and case studies around the world. For instance, the Green School in Bali exemplifies how integrating sustainability into education can lead to significant environmental and social impacts. Such examples underscore the potential of ESD to foster active and engaged citizens who contribute to sustainable development at both local and global levels.

Moreover, empirical studies underscore the positive outcomes of ESD on student behaviour and community engagement. Students who participate in ESD programs are more likely to engage in sustainable practices, demonstrating the transformative potential of education in promoting sustainability. In conclusion, education is a powerful catalyst for sustainable development, capable of driving profound changes in individual behaviours and societal norms.

By fostering critical thinking, promoting holistic understanding, and empowering individuals to take responsible actions, ESD can significantly contribute to building a sustainable and equitable future. Continued investment in and commitment to ESD are essential to overcoming current challenges and realizing its full potential in promoting global sustainability.

References:

1. Barth, M., Godemann, J., Rieckmann, M., & Stoltenberg, U. (2007). Developing key competencies for sustainable development in higher education. *International Journal of Sustainability in Higher Education*, 8(4), 416-430.

2. Biasutti, M., & Frate, S. (2017). A validity and reliability study of the Attitudes Toward Sustainable Development scale. *Environmental Education Research*, 23(2), 214-230.

3. de Haan, G. (2006). The BLK '21' programme in Germany: A 'Gestaltungskompetenz'-based model for Education for Sustainable Development. *Environmental Education Research*, 12(1), 19-32.

4. Mezirow, J. (1997). Transformative learning: Theory to practice. New Directions for Adult and Continuing Education, 1997(74), 5-12.

5. Green School Bali. (2020). *Green School Bali: Empowering global citizens and green leaders.* Retrieved from https://www.greenschool.org

6. Sterling, S. (2010). Transformative learning and sustainability: Sketching the conceptual ground. *Learning and Teaching in Higher Education*, 5, 17-33.

7. Tilbury, D. (2011). Education for sustainable development: An expert review of processes and learning. *UNESCO.*

8. UNESCO. (2014). *Shaping the Future We Want: UN Decade of Education for Sustainable Development (2005-2014) Final Report.* Paris: UNESCO.

9. UNESCO. (2017). *Education for Sustainable Development Goals: Learning Objectives.* Paris: UNESCO.

10. United Nations (UN). (1992). *Agenda 21.* Retrieved from https://sustainabledevelopment.un.org/content/documents/Agenda21.pdf

11. United Nations (UN). (2015). *Transforming our world: the 2030 Agenda for Sustainable Development.* Retrieved from https://sustainabledevelopment.un.org/post2015/transformingourworld.

12. Wikimedia Commons. (n.d.). *Dimensions of* Sustainable development. Retrieved from https://upload.wikimedia.org/wikipedia/commons/7/70/Sustainable_development.svg

13. Wiek, A., Withycombe, L., & Redman, C. L. (2011). Key competencies in sustainability: A reference framework for academic program development. Sustainability Science, 6(2), 203-218.

3. Advancements in Food Technology for Reducing Food Waste

Dt. Deepika Sharma

Clinical Dietician/ Nutritionist

Udaipur, (Raj.)

Email: deepikasharma5979@gmail.com

Abstract:

Food waste affects the environment, society, and economy worldwide, making it a serious problem. Startling figures are highlighted in reports from the United Nations Environment Programme (UNEP) and other sources: 40% of food produced in the US is wasted, while 68.7 million tonnes of food are wasted annually in Indian households. This waste increases food insecurity and adds to greenhouse gas emissions. New developments in food technology present encouraging answers to this issue. Extending shelf life, minimizing spoiling, and guaranteeing food safety are all made possible by smart packaging, which includes active and intelligent packaging. Food preservation techniques like Pulsed Electric Fields (PEF) and High-Pressure Processing (HPP) preserve food's nutritional value and sensory attributes while increasing its shelf life. Innovations in food processing, such as repurposing food waste and sophisticated.

Keywords: Packaging, food waste, smart packaging, food technology.

1. Introduction:

Food waste is a serious worldwide problem that influences the economy, society, and environment. The United Nations Environment Programme's (UNEP) food waste index report states that 68.7 million tonnes of food, or roughly 55 kg per person, are wasted annually in Indian households. In terms of food waste in households, it is ranked second in the world, only behind China. According to a National Resources Defence Council (NDRC) report, 40% of food produced in the US is wasted, while 1.34 billion tonnes of food are wasted in Asia, with China and India being the two biggest contributors. (Agriculture,2024). This contributes to greenhouse gas emissions and food insecurity in addition to being an enormous waste of resources. This not only represents a colossal waste of resources but also contributes to greenhouse gas emissions and food insecurity. In recent years, advancements in food technology have emerged as a promising avenue to tackle this problem.

The four basic functions of packaging are generally protection, communication, convenience, and containment. It also serves to separate the products from the external environment. With useful features like the ability to microwave or reclose products, it makes handling them easier for the customer and communicates with them through written texts or graphics. In addition, it accommodates the lifestyle of the customer and provides a variety of sizes and shapes for the containers. Packaging not only enhances marketing and distribution but also reduces deterioration in quality. For this reason, they play a vital role in the secure transportation and preservation of packaged food. It is not feasible to eradicate the quality loss, though. Highly perishable foods undergo intrinsic property changes during processing. This may result in a loss of quality or an improvement in quality (such as fruits reaching a specific level of ripeness): The product may spoil due to biological, chemical, or physical processes that arise from the contents of the package. In most cases, consumers find it challenging to evaluate these changes. Many shoppers discard goods that would have otherwise been fit for consumption out of concern that their groceries may go bad. Frequently, a minor deviance from the standard, concerning color, consistency, or even the expiration date, results in products being thrown away (Müller and Schmid, 2019).

Seven categories exist for food packaging materials and containers: composite packaging, paper, glass, ceramic, metal, plastic, and other packaging. Because it is inexpensive, lightweight, and portable, plastic packaging is frequently used for tea, fruit juice, and other products. Paper packaging materials are inexpensive, offer good protection, and are simple to use. Recycling, as well as paper bags and cartons. Glass packaging is used in storage tanks, glass tableware, grain and oil bottles, and other applications because of its good and consistent chemical stability and barrier qualities. A lot of everyday items are made of ceramic, and metal packaging materials help keep food from deteriorating, spoiling, or changing flavor. Currently, milk powder and canned meat are the two main uses for metal food packaging materials.

These days, intelligent food packaging has emerged to meet consumer demands for food safety and quality while reducing needless food waste. In general, food products' exteriors and interiors can be felt, examined, and tracked by intelligent packaging, which can provide additional details on the quality of the food. From the supply of raw materials to the manufacturing, packaging, distribution, and sale of the products, as well as the disposal of packaging waste and other information-related functions like sensing, storing, transmitting, and feedback functions, intelligent food packaging may realize the food processing process. (Ma et al., 2022).

Clever packaging Improved communication of changes in food within the package and the display of multiple alerts of possible issues in the package's environment that shows food quality about time, temperature, sensors, freshness, integrity, and so forth, pH, or volatile substances related to food deterioration or microorganism growth are examples of the technologies being used to improve food quality awareness (Vasuki et al., 2023). To ensure food safety before it reaches consumers, intelligent packaging combines traditional packaging with sophisticated electronic sensing devices like sensors to detect changes in food quality. On the other hand, active packaging adds active ingredients like antioxidants to conventional packaging materials to improve food stability and quality over the course of the product's shelf life (Drago et al., 2020).

2. Smart Packaging:

Smart packaging technologies are revolutionizing the way food products are stored, transported, and monitored. These advancements help extend the shelf life of perishable goods, reduce spoilage, and enhance food safety.

2.1. Active Packaging: Active packaging involves materials that interact with the food product to maintain or improve its condition. This can include oxygen scavengers, ethylene absorbers, and antimicrobial agents. For example, oxygen scavengers prevent the oxidation of sensitive products like meats and dairy, thereby extending their shelf life.

2.2. Intelligent Packaging: Intelligent packaging systems provide real-time information about the condition of the food product. Sensors embedded in packaging materials can detect temperature changes, humidity levels, and the presence of gases indicative of spoilage. QR codes and RFID tags can also offer consumers and retailers information on the product's freshness and optimal usage periods.

3. Preservation Technologies:

Advancements in preservation technologies are crucial for extending the shelf life of food products and reducing waste.

3.1. High-Pressure Processing (HPP): High-pressure processing (HPP) is a non-thermal preservation method that uses high pressure to inactivate pathogens and spoilage microorganisms. HPP retains the sensory and nutritional qualities of food better than traditional thermal methods, making it an attractive option for preserving juices, ready-to-eat meals, and seafood.

3.2. Pulsed Electric Fields (PEF): Pulsed Electric Fields (PEF) technology applies short bursts of high voltage to food products, disrupting cell membranes and inactivating microorganisms. PEF is effective in extending the shelf life of liquid foods like juices and milk without significantly affecting their taste or nutritional value.

4. Food Processing Innovations:

Innovative food processing methods are essential for maximizing the use of raw materials and reducing by-products that contribute to waste.

4.1. Upcycling Food Waste: Upcycling involves converting food waste into value-added products. Technologies have been developed to transform fruit peels, vegetable trimmings, and other by-products into functional ingredients, such as dietary fibers, natural colorants, and bioactive compounds. For instance, citrus peel can be processed into pectin, a valuable gelling agent used in food production.

4.2. Advanced Drying Techniques: Advanced drying techniques, such as freeze-drying and spray-drying, help preserve surplus produce by reducing its moisture content and extending its shelf life. These methods retain the nutritional quality and flavor of the food, making them suitable for creating high-quality dried fruits, vegetables, and powdered ingredients.

5. Digital Solutions and Artificial Intelligence:

Digital technologies and artificial intelligence (AI) are playing a transformative role in optimizing food production, distribution, and consumption processes to minimize waste.

5.1. Predictive Analytics: AI-powered predictive analytics can forecast demand more accurately, helping producers and retailers manage inventory more efficiently. By analyzing data on consumer behavior, weather patterns, and market trends, AI systems can reduce overproduction and ensure that food reaches consumers before it spoils.

5.2. Supply Chain Optimization: Blockchain technology and Internet of Things (IoT) devices enhance traceability and transparency in the food supply chain. These technologies enable real-time tracking of food products, ensuring optimal storage conditions and timely distribution. This reduces the likelihood of food spoilage during transportation and storage.

6. Consumer Engagement and Education:

Technological advancements also focus on engaging and educating consumers to reduce food waste at the household level.

6.1. Mobile Apps and Platforms: Mobile apps and online platforms provide consumers with tools to manage their food inventory, plan meals, and find creative uses for leftovers. Apps like "Too Good To Go" and "OLIO" connect consumers with surplus food from restaurants and retailers at discounted prices, promoting a culture of waste reduction.

6.2. Smart Refrigerators: Smart refrigerators equipped with cameras and inventory management systems help households keep track of their food supplies. These appliances can suggest recipes based on available ingredients, remind users of expiration dates, and even create shopping lists to avoid overbuying.

7. Conclusion:

A comprehensive approach that incorporates consumer education, technology innovation, and structural improvements in food production and distribution is required to combat food waste. The key to reducing food waste is the development of smart packaging, preservation technology, creative food processing techniques, digital solutions, and customer involvement. These technologies optimize resource usage and boost supply chain efficiency in addition to extending the shelf life of food goods and improving food safety. By offering real-time insights into food quality and condition, active and intelligent packaging solutions minimize needless discards because of apparent spoiling. Food preservation techniques such as Pulsed Electric Fields (PEF) and High-Pressure Processing (HPP) preserve food's nutritional value and sensory attributes while successfully prolonging its shelf life. Innovations in food processing, like repurposing food scraps and using cutting-edge.

References:

1. Agriculture, T. O. (2024, May 29). *Food wastage in India 2024: From farm to bin, Hidden truth*. Times of Agriculture: e-Magazine. https://timesofagriculture.in/food-wastage-in-india-farm-tobin/#:~:text=In%20India%2C%2040%25%20of%20the,per%20UN%20Environment%20Programme's%20report.
2. Müller, P., & Schmid, M. (2019). Intelligent Packaging in the food sector: A Brief Overview. *Foods, 8*(1), 16. https://doi.org/10.3390/foods8010016
3. Ma, Y., Yang, W., Xia, Y., Xue, W., Wu, H., Li, Z., Zhang, F., Qiu, B., & Fu, C. (2022). Properties and Applications of Intelligent Packaging Indicators for food Spoilage. *Membranes, 12*(5), 477. https://doi.org/10.3390/membranes12050477

4. Drago, E., Campardelli, R., Pettinato, M., & Perego, P. (2020). Innovations in Smart Packaging Concepts for Food: An Extensive review. *Foods*, *9*(11), 1628. https://doi.org/10.3390/foods9111628

5. Vasuki, M. T., Kadirvel, V., & Narayana, G. P. (2023). Smart packaging—An overview of concepts and applications in various food industries. *Food Bioengineering*, *2*(1), 25–41. https://doi.org/10.1002/fbe2.12038

4. The Socio-Economic Benefits of Urban Green Spaces: A Systematic Review

Pranoy Dey

Assistant Professor, Department of Geography, Birpara College

Alipurduar, West Bengal, Pin- 735204

Email: pranoy.dey93@gmail.com

Abstract:

In recent times, the concept of creating green cities has gained worldwide recognition. This approach seeks to tackle the challenges posed by increased urbanization, population expansion, and climate change. Urban green spaces (UGS) are crucial assets that can assist cities in mitigating the negative impacts of rapid urbanization and urban sprawl in a sustainable manner. Urban green spaces serve a crucial role in cities by acting as a source of oxygen, reducing urban heat, acting as a barrier against dangerous air pollution, and providing considerable environmental, social, and economic advantages to the city. Nevertheless, the significance of underground gas storage (UGS) as a crucial sector in urban design is consistently overlooked. However, while being widely appreciated, UGS is often seen as a problem and not considered a valuable asset in the planning and development process. Therefore, the objective of this study is to comprehend the numerous advantages of developing urban green spaces within the context of modern urban sustainability discourse.

Keywords: Urban Green Space, Urbanization, Climate Change, Socio Economic Benefits, Sustainability

1. Introduction:

Urban green spaces offer a diverse variety of applications and has a substantial impact on an urban environment. They play a crucial role in creating peaceful urban environments by mitigating environmental stress, reducing excessive noise, and alleviating traffic congestion. The primary strategy to counteract the negative impacts of fast urbanization and urban sprawl in a sustainable manner is to prioritize the expansion of green spaces in metropolitan areas. The research on the advantages of urban green space has garnered significant interest from numerous experts. Western researchers prioritize the assessment of urban green space (UGS) quality, as defined by Miller (2005), who has classified the functions and quality of UGS into three categories: engineering function, architectural and beautifying function, and environmental and climatic function. Recently, scholars worldwide, both in the western and Asian regions, have been influenced by the notion of sustainable development approach

(Cilliers, 2017). Various analyses have extensively discussed the advantages of underground gas storage (UGS) by categorizing them into three sustainable development goals: improving social conditions, safeguarding the environment, and promoting economic expansion. Regrettably, the sustainability agenda introduces new tangible goods to the urban green space (UGS). However, in recent times, particularly in compact cities, the value of green space is often underestimated in the planning and development process (Waldner, 2009). The limited availability of land in urban areas has highlighted the role of green spaces as a barrier to development. In the present day, urban areas are becoming densely populated. Humans have significantly altered and transformed the natural landscape. The influx of unregulated people into urban areas results in the alteration of land utilization patterns (Awang Besar et al., 2014). Urbanization is a significant phenomenon that results in the concentration of people in urban areas and the alteration of land cover. In 2016, more than half (54.5 percent) of the global population lived in cities such as Tokyo, Delhi, and Hong Kong. There was a total of 31 megacities worldwide, each with over 10 million residents. Out of these, 15 were located in Asia and Africa (UN, 2016).

Urbanization has caused increased pressure and reduced the size of green spaces in many cities in Asia, North and South America, and Africa (Abebe & Megento, 2016). The desire for new housing and contemporary infrastructure in the city has led to the generation of this (Kabisch et al., 2016). The conversion of natural vegetation into impermeable surfaces due to urbanization has the most significant impact. The once verdant area has been completely transformed into a dark, impenetrable surface, entirely covered with concrete and asphalt. It is evident that there is no remaining space for any form of vegetation to thrive (Jiang & Tian, 2010). Consequently, this leads to alterations in the structure, configuration, and dimensions of the city, which are referred to as the presence of urban growth (M. Nor et al., 2017). According to his analysis, one of the reasons for the transformation of the city's shape is the weak policy framework and inadequate implementation of urban monitoring management. The absence of a well-coordinated master plan, coupled with insufficient knowledge for future initiatives, has hindered the development of the green space planning system.

2. Benefits of Urban Green Spaces:

The absence of green spaces, especially in metropolitan settings, is akin to a loss of our essence and humanity. The obstacles to the establishment of underground storage (UGS) are only associated with minimal harm to the environment and can be altered via human empowerment.

However, neglecting its importance in the planning process would result in a loss for the global ecology. The green spaces in a city are naturally designed to enhance the quality of life for humanity. Envision a metropolis devoid of any green areas, completely dominated by a concrete jungle where there is little room for leisure activities or personal connection, resulting in a high likelihood of experiencing anxiety and discontent. Hence, it is imperative for us to comprehend and value the existence of urban green spaces and their role in enhancing the city's environment, as well as contributing to social and economic development.

2.1. Environmental Benefits:

2.1.1. Improve Urban Climate: Several scientists, particularly from Asia, have documented that the existence of urban green spaces (UGS) can mitigate the intensity of heat in the surrounding environment, decrease wind velocity, enhance precipitation, and facilitate cities in adapting to climate change (Isa et al., 2017; Kim et al., 2016; Liu & Shen, 2014). Urban areas with impermeable surfaces, such as asphalt, concrete, bricks, and stone, have a lower thermal capacity. As a result, they absorb a greater amount of radiation energy from the sun. These factors contribute to an increase in energy usage and result in varying temperature patterns in metropolitan areas, leading to the occurrence of metropolitan Heat Islands (UHI) phenomena. Extensive research has demonstrated that green spaces in urban settings can function as natural cooling agents, known as Green Space Cool Island (GCI) or Urban Cool Island (UCI) (Buyadi et al., 2014; Du et al., 2017). Liu and Shen (2014) conducted study that demonstrated a high correlation between the size, shape, and types of green space patches and a reduction in temperature in the Taipei Metropolitan region. The aggregation of urban green spaces has a strong association with the temperature in this metropolis, affecting the pattern of rainfall and reducing the air pollution index.

The study conducted by Buyadi et al. (2014) found that the proportion of urban green spaces (UGS) was the most influential factor in reducing hot temperatures in the Shah Alam area, Malaysia. The study's analysis reveals that places with a high concentration of green space have a much lower temperature of 25.8°C, compared to built-up areas which have a temperature increase of 30.8°C. By strategically incorporating new parks and protecting forest areas, urban expansion can effectively mitigate the air temperature in a metropolis.

2.1.2. Eliminate Noise and Reduction of Air Pollutants: Soft walls are recognized as inherent obstacles for noise pollution. Not only does it serve as a border shape and beauty aspect, but it also functions as noise isolators (Nezar, 2010). When there are thousands of motor vehicles in urban places like Beijing, China, the noise they make can reach high decibel levels. This can have negative impacts on the health of the residents, particularly when the noise exceeds 70 decibels (Manlun, 2003). This can be achieved by implementing a 4.4-meter wide green belt between the UGS facility and the source of the disruptive sound (Haq, 2011). One of the most cost-effective approaches to reduce noise pollution is by providing an adequate amount of green space in a busy city. Air pollution has a substantial impact on human health, particularly for those living in metropolitan areas who struggle to breathe in clean oxygen (Lee & Maheswaran, 2017). His literary analysis revealed a correlation between decreased exposure to green spaces and increased stroke death rates. Conversely, in 2012, the World Health Organization (WHO) projected that approximately 3.7 million deaths were caused by excessive exposure to outdoor air pollution resulting from transportation, energy, waste management, and industrial operations. According to Desikan's (2017) findings, individuals residing within a distance of less than 100 meters from high traffic zones saw a mortality rate that was 20% higher compared to those living within a distance of less than 400 meters. The study reveals that air pollution, namely including small particulate matter (PM) with a diameter of less than 2.5 µm, has the capacity to penetrate deeper into the lungs and increase stroke mortality and morbidity. These occurrences were observed in urban locations. Green areas not only serve as aesthetic components, but they also have the ability to enhance the air quality of a city. According to Mohd Noor et al. (2013), a single tree has the capacity to remove 26 pounds of carbon dioxide annually, which is equivalent to the emissions produced by driving a car for 11,000 kilometers. Therefore, it is imperative to dedicate a greater number of green spaces in urban settings in order to purify the air that is being breathed, and these areas should be regarded as very valuable assets to the cities.

2.1.3. Natural Hydrological Management: The rapid advancements in construction techniques and the use of non-permeable surfaces lead to an increase in the volume and speed of water runoff. This, in turn, results in flooding, erosion, and a decline in water quality (Mohd Yusof, 2012). The study conducted by M'Ikiugu et al. (2012) involved the distribution of 121 questionnaires among respondents from municipalities and neighborhoods in Tokyo. They unanimously acknowledged that green areas have a significant value of 4.51 out of 5 in terms of their role in disaster prevention and lowering run-off through greater penetration. The temporary water storage capacity will retain the water until it can be released and reused by urban dwellers. In addition, a study conducted by Kim et al. (2016) in Seoul, Korea found that the presence of green spaces in places with mild slopes can lead to a reduction of over 50% in flooding volume. The extent of this reduction depends on the types of green spaces and their specific locations where they are implemented. Hence, it is imperative for emerging nations to conserve and oversee the green spaces with the same level of importance as other forms of land utilization.

2.1.4. A 'Home' for Biodiversity Growth: Myers et al., (2013) state that the millennium development goals have significantly altered almost all of the natural land. The degradation of the ecosystem persists, with limited focus on the potential impact to human health resulting from these natural processes. According to Myers, deforestation has significantly increased the risk of infectious diseases, such as malaria, in Africa by reducing the population sizes of species. The increased quantity of green space will enhance biodiversity by preserving a greater variety of species and landscape types in the surrounding areas. This will also help in the conservation of green space, as opposed to smaller fragmented patches (M. Nor et al., 2017). Urban and regional planning should prioritize the protection of urban green spaces to support habitats for desired species and promote community efforts to increase biodiversity on their land. This can be achieved by providing training, appropriate tools, and sufficient funding.

2.2. Social and Psychological Benefits:

2.2.1. A Place for Human Interaction and Integration: The principle of inclusivity in planning theory is clearly evident in the spatial organization of areas that aim to promote societal values and interests in the development of Urban Green Spaces (UGS) (Van Herzele & Wiedemann, 2003). Mansor & Said, (2008) found that locals in Taiping, Malaysia utilize green spaces as a meeting place to strengthen community bonds, such as through organizing community sports events. The contact will generate new integration among the users of the green space through physical experiences. Roberts, (2017) utilized Twitter data to gain insights into the utilization of UGS (Urban Green Spaces) locations in relation to human interactions. According to a survey, the majority of visitors to Cannon Hill Park and Sparkhill Park in England utilize Twitter as a means to entice people to participate in various activities such as music festivals, culinary festivals, and summer fetes. These events foster integration, particularly among young individuals from diverse backgrounds and cultures, allowing them to welcome one another. The free marketing and promotion offered by Twitter can greatly enhance the utilization of UGS and facilitate meaningful human interactions.

A recent study conducted in Hong Kong and Singapore has revealed an intriguing discovery: the spatial configuration of urban green spaces (UGS) can have an impact on human interactions. A location that offers a greater number of shaded amenities and a diverse range of landscapes will enhance people's desire to stay for longer periods of time and engage in social networking activities with greater comfort. In their 2012 study, Marzukhi et al. found that the size of green spaces should be sufficient to accommodate the population's requirements in terms of the variety and concentration of neighborhood areas. The strategic placement of green areas is crucial for maximizing the beneficial impacts of community social interactions and enjoyment.

2.2.2. Outdoor Fitness and Health Improvement: UGS can serve as a natural fitness facility. The city provides a diverse array of locations where residents can engage in various physical activities for their exercise. Lee & Maheswaran, (2017) found that residents tend to use green spaces more often when they are easily accessible and located near neighboring neighborhoods. Individuals are more likely to engage in physical exercise with their family and friends when there are less obstacles to accessing green places. This factor will impact the utilization of green spaces and consequently impact the improvement of social networking activity. Mansor and Harun (2014) assert that the proximity of green spaces to one's residence enhances individuals' motivation to engage in physical activity and maintain their overall well-being. A variety of green spaces, including parks, playing fields, jogging trails, and tree-lined avenues, are available near the residential areas. These green spaces enhance the residents' well-being and allow them to enjoy outdoor fitness activities.

Stigsdotter, (2014) observed that those who regularly access or visit even a modest garden experience fewer stressful events. There is a strong correlation between the amount of time spent in green spaces and an individual's health state. The study also discovered that individuals in the workplace who have exposure to or the opportunity to experience an outdoor setting exhibit lower levels of anger and depression, hence demonstrating a higher level of job quality.

2.3. Economic Benefits:

2.3.1. A Valuable Asset to Economy Improvement: According to Chiesura, (2004), the existence of green spaces in a city is advantageous not only for the people living around them, but also for the municipalities responsible for managing, controlling, and planning these green spaces, who will also gain equally. Mohd Noor et al., (2015) asserted that properties within a

400-meter radius of green spaces experience a price increase ranging from 3 to 12 percent. A study employing hedonic valuation modeling was conducted to assess property values in Subang Jaya, Selangor. The study revealed that the proximity to green spaces significantly affects the range of land values. The Department of Environment, Land, Water, and Planning of Canada conducted a study in 2004 to identify and measure the various economic benefits of green spaces. It is asserted that properties located within a 200-meter radius of green areas had a 4.4 percent increase in their price. The presence of a tree canopy also contributes to an increase in the retail value. It is intriguing to learn that individuals in the Victoria area, Canada are willing to pay a premium of 9 to 12 percent for goods when the retail operation is situated under a high-quality tree canopy. The reason for their extended stay and comfort is why they are willing to pay for both the products and the atmosphere. A compelling study conducted by Santos et al., (2016) asserts that green areas in Philadelphia, PA, USA can serve as natural disaster protection measures and provide numerous advantages to inhabitants. This is due to the fact that local governments are providing a diverse range of financial resources and support to those who are capable of effectively managing and preserving their green spaces. Residents have the opportunity to apply for lower stormwater taxes and get financial incentives as a reward for preserving the "valuable assets." According to the United States Environmental Protection Agency (EPA) in 2014, trees can decrease homeowners' air conditioning costs by 15-50 percent. Green spaces can function as a natural cooling mechanism for human comfort. KL and Singapore provide as examples that support Haq's, (2011) assertion that the presence of green spaces throughout a city's boundaries is a significant element in attracting foreign investments. It is believed that the financial and property worth will experience a boost of 5 to 15 percent when new projects are created in close proximity to natural spaces. According to Crompton, (2011), a park that provides passive activities, gorgeous scenery, is well-maintained, and has less noise might potentially improve house prices by 20%. Nevertheless, the price of the new house complexes located near the popular park, which offers various recreational facilities such as athletic fields and a swimming pool, may be reduced by up to 10%. In China, the range of housing prices for flats is influenced by the availability of nearby green spaces and the provision of scenic views of water bodies and vegetation for the tenants (Jim & Chen, 2006). Residences located in close proximity to green facilities command higher prices and are highly sought after.

2.3.2. Beautification and Attractive: In 1996, the Social Program and Sustainable Development Department in Washington, D.C. established a framework for implementing effective strategies in urban greening. According to them, green spaces can have a considerable impact on enhancing the visual appeal of the city and consequently boost the feeling of civic pride. They believe that green spaces have the ability to mitigate the urban landscape and counteract the starkness of the concrete hue. A study conducted by Valipoor & Dehkordi, (2016) in Tehran revealed that the majority of citizens strongly believe that the existence of urban green spaces enhances the beauty and attractiveness of their city. They advocate for the authorities to enhance the importance of green spaces by increasing their aesthetic value beyond what is currently provided. This demonstrates that humans have an inherent inclination towards appreciating beauty, and the presence of green spaces is one of the contributing aspects that enhance human well-being and vitality.

3. Green Spaces as Safety Tools:

According to a study conducted by Kuo & Sullivian, (2001), the presence of greenery has the ability to decrease crime through many methods and strategies. This study indicates that there is an inverse relationship between the amount of greenery in buildings and the occurrence of crime. In other words, as the amount of greenery increases, the number of crimes decreases. The reason is that people are inclined to engage in outdoor activities together, which creates a more vibrant atmosphere and deters criminals. This study also discovered that apartment complexes situated in close proximity to natural spaces experienced a significant 48 percent reduction in crime cases compared to other places. Locke et al., (2017) also express a similar worry, stating that implementing neighborhood greening initiatives in New Haven, Connecticut, could potentially contribute to a decrease in crime rates. The active involvement of community members in initiatives such as expanding street tree planting in public areas, beautifying abandoned property, and improving private yards significantly reduces the likelihood of crime in their neighborhood. Nevertheless, many researchers have asserted that areas with thick vegetation or green spaces may serve as a breeding ground for criminal behavior (Fisher & Nasar, 1992; Michael et al., 2001). The offenders often utilize the green spaces block as a hiding spot before committing acts of vandalism, such as breaking windows. The hypothesis of "broken window," as articulated by Wilson and Kelling in 1982, posits that areas with evident overgrowth of bushes and trees can serve as conducive environments for criminals to evade detection. Hence, it is imperative to carefully evaluate the appropriate planning, design, and placement of green spaces in order to establish a complete strategy for crime reduction through environmental design. Green spaces have the potential to not only decrease crime rates, but also to decrease or impede traffic flow.

4. Barriers of Urban Green Spaces:

The significance of urban green spaces (UGS) has been recognized for several decades, as evidenced by numerous reviews that attribute a great deal of credit to green spaces for enhancing the atmosphere of cities, improving the well-being of urban residents, and generating positive economic benefits in a sustainable manner. The hardscape is not only perceived as a natural area designed for recreational activities, but it also serves other functions that go beyond our evaluation. Several studies have asserted that the existence of urban green spaces (UGS) can effectively mitigate urban heat islands and enhance various aspects of a city, such as its temperature, air quality, and biodiversity. Nevertheless, to what extent does the urban green space persist and contribute to the overall sustainability of the city? While UGS may be highly regarded by everyone, it might become a burden and be considered as non-commodity goods during the development phase (Mohd Noor et al., 2015).

4.1. Cost of Maintenance: The financial burden of upkeeping green areas within a city poses a difficulty for the local governing body (Ibrahim, 2016). Based on his research, the swift process of urbanization has led to a higher requirement for advanced infrastructure and large-scale amenities to meet the needs of the city's people. Ensuring the provision and maintenance of green spaces is essential, especially in cases when local councils receive little or no financial return. Consequently, the tax revenue's allocation budget is mostly directed towards infrastructure development and facility enhancement, rather than being used for the creation or maintenance of green spaces. In addition, the intangible benefits provided by green space are often overlooked, and occasionally the budget needs to be reduced in order to prioritize revenue-generating improvements (Cilliers, 2015).

In a 2014 survey on public parks in the UK, it was said that 45% of local governments are contemplating the sale of their green spaces due to the financial burden associated with maintenance expenses. The researchers discovered that the annual cost of maintaining urban parks ranges from 0.28 to 1.34 euros per square meter. The continual upkeep of the area, which includes the expenses of replanting and removing plants, as well as the costs of human resources and management fees, results in a burden for the local government. Ibrahim, (2016) emphasizes that the local government is responsible for the maintenance cost of parks once the developers have completed the master plan projects. Despite the planning guidelines mandating a specific quantity of green space in a master plan, the lack of personnel for technical upkeep and limited budget allocation for green spaces has led to inadequate greening areas. These will enhance the possibility for the utilization of green spaces as a valuable land use activity. Haaland & Bosch, (2015) argue that the supply of green areas in cities experiencing densification is a highly disputed and discussed issue, mostly due to financial constraints. He is sceptical of the subpar greening due to its lack of upkeep and insufficient investment, which has resulted in the abandonment of unused area. This will ensure that the conversion of green spaces into more profitable sectors leads to an increase in impervious surfaces within a metropolis.

4.2. Land Ownership: Land tenure may provide a major barrier to implementing urban greening initiatives in numerous places (Sorensen, 1997). According to his research, the ownership and management of land by individuals is a complex task, and the general public is unlikely to take care of trees or plants placed on it due to legal restrictions. However, it is usual for private landowners to prioritize developing the region for more profitable purposes rather than preserving it as natural resources. In addition, they encounter the budgeted maintenance cost, sources of revenue, and tax payments. This refers to a distinct scenario involving land owned by the government, which is specifically designated for protection and preservation. These sites receive an annual budget allocation for upkeep, technical assistance to ensure cleanliness, and various services to maintain their beauty. The lack of sophistication in the development of private urban green spaces in a metropolis has hindered the connection between citizens and nature. The issue of limited public access to urban green spaces due to fragmented private property ownership leads to misconceptions about the availability of green spaces in their areas (Derkzen et al., 2017). These actions represent social changes that cause urban green spaces to become mono-functional and nonfunctional. They also reinforce the belief among citizens that green spaces are primarily meant to cater to the demands and benefits of high-class communities.

Mensah, (2014) argues that the ownership of land has led to significant devastation of green areas in Kumasi, Ghana. The surplus property owned by individuals with political connections to the government has undergone significant transformation into new development. Despite the presence of high-risk development zones like as nature reserves, there is a lack of supervision, protection, and progress without compound. The reason for this is that chiefs, who are the traditional leaders in the community authorities, have jurisdiction over 60% of the green space areas in Kumasi, but the local council of the city does not have control over them. Consequently, the contradictory regulatory authority governing the allocation of green spaces has hindered the Ghanaian government's endeavours to safeguard its natural reserve areas due to issues surrounding property ownership rights.

5. Conclusion:

It is imperative for both local authorities and government administrations to prioritize and actively pursue the development of green spaces. In order to effectively participate in the city development process, the green space must align itself with the other land use sectors. It should be seen as a commodity and be considered as a profitable asset for the city's growth. In addition to the advantages that green spaces provide to the overall planning system in terms of social and economic aspects, they also play a crucial role in preserving the environment for future generations. Green space not only enhances our health by improving air quality and reducing noise pollution, but it also serves as a means to stabilize the ambiance of our city. It has the potential to function as a generator that can decrease heat in a metropolis, mitigate the speed of run-off, and serve as a habitat for our biodiversity. To enhance the value and functionality of the green space, it is necessary to allocate it more precisely based on the specific needs of the community, the type of space, and the features of the neighborhood. The formulation and development of guidelines and policy should involve many levels of community background. For example, the division of open space into public and private areas should be eliminated. The functionality, services, links, and facilities are designed to be similar and parallel, while also respecting individual rights. Furthermore, private landowners should receive additional incentives such as tax exemptions, reduced fees, and grants to encourage them to preserve the lands and distribute the resulting advantages to the wider community. As a result, it will generate a more diverse environment instead of uniform green areas. Individuals will have a greater sense of inclusivity, unity, and ease in interacting with others of all levels. In the context of urbanization, the presence of green space may not always be the most effective strategy to achieve sufficient environmental sustainability due to the limited availability of land. Nevertheless, this is not a sufficient justification for eradicating its existence within a metropolis. Establishing new parks in urban areas might incur significant costs. To save maintenance expenses and tax burdens, planners can employ more innovative strategies, such as transforming unused sections into green spaces. Enhancing the structure and function of the grey area might transform it into green space. Grey space refers to impermeable surfaces such as highways, buildings, parking lots, and other concrete structures found in a metropolis. While the large grey areas in the city may seem significant, it is more advantageous to allocate part of these places for vegetation purposes rather than creating a new park on a single piece of land.

Grey infrastructure tends to require less land, can be replicated, and is relatively easier to monitor and govern. For instance, in New York City, the former rails have been transformed into a linear public park including of green areas and cultural facilities. The New York City Planning Commission granted approval on September 20, 2012, to modify the land use zoning text for the High Rail Line, transforming it into a public park. In 2015, the collaboration of the local governments, park's board landscape, and the community resulted in an increase of the annual budget for maintenance, facilities, and beautification to 98% (NYC EDC, 2016). This study presents a challenge for urban planners and urban landscape designers to create a more robust urban fabric. The development of green spaces within a city should take into consideration the cultural and spatial design context of the community. The implementation of human rights and authority has the potential to overcome the challenges associated with the development of green spaces. However, disregarding the advantages of green spaces would be detrimental to the entire ecosystem. This type of limitation is a minor form of damage that may be mitigated by making adjustments, fostering creativity, and creating a sense of unity. These actions can have a good impact on culture, human behaviour, and transform our environment into a more green and sustainable setting.

References:

1. Abebe, M. T., & Megento, T. L. (2016). THE CITY OF ADDIS ABABA FROM'FOREST CITY'TO'URBAN HEAT ISLAND' ASSESSMENT OF URBAN GREEN SPACE DYNAMICS. *Journal of Urban and Environmental Engineering,10*(2), 254-262.

2. Baharuddin, Z.M., Sivam, A., Karuppannan, S., Daniels, C.B., (2010). Urban Green Space: Stakeholders' and Visitors' Perception in Kuala Lumpur Malaysia. *Making Cities Liveable*, 15–26.

3. Besar, J. A., Fauzi, R., Ghazali, A. S., Ghani, M. H. A., & Baharum, Z. A. (2014). Kuala Lumpur dan cabaran baru pembangunan berterusan. *Geografia-Malaysian Journal of Society and Space,10*(6), 75-85.

4. Buyadi, S. N. A., Mohd, W. M. N. W., & Misni, A. (2014). Quantifying green space cooling effects on the urban microclimate using remote sensing and gis techniques. *Proceedings of the XXV International Federation of Surveyors*, 1-16.

5. Canada Government. (2004). Green Space Acquisition and Stewardship in Canada's Urban Municipalities Canada.

6. Chiesura, A. (2004). The role of urban parks for the sustainable city. *Landscape and urban planning,68*(1), 129-138.

7. Cilliers, E.J., (2017). The Importance of Planning for Green Spaces, (April).

8. Crompton, J. L. (2001). Perceptions of how the presence of greenway trails affects the value of proximate properties. *Journal of Park and Recreation Administration, 19*(3), 114-132.

9. Davidson, M., & Dolnick, F. (2004). *A planner dictionary. Chicago: Planning Advisory Service, PAS*(No. 521/522). Report.

10. DBKL., (2017). Kuala Lumpur Annual Budget Report 2017. Kuala Lumpur City Hall, Kuala Lumpur. DBKL., 2013. Kuala Lumpur City Plan 2020. Kuala Lumpur City Hall, Kuala Lumpur.

11. In: Kabisch N., Korn H., Stadler J., Bonn A. (eds) Nature-Based Solutions to Climate Change Adaptation in Urban Areas. Theory and Practice of Urban Sustainability Transitions. Springer, Cham.

12. Depietri, Y., & McPhearson, T. (2017). Integrating the grey, green, and blue in cities: Nature-based solutions for climate change adaptation and risk reduction. *Nature-based solutions to climate change adaptation in urban areas: Linkages between science, policy and practice*, 91-109.

13. Derkzen, M. L., van Teeffelen, A. J., Nagendra, H., & Verburg, P. H. (2017). Shifting roles of urban green space in the context of urban development and global change. *Current Opinion in Environmental Sustainability, 29*, 32-39.

14. Desikan, A. (2017). Outdoor air pollution as a possible modifiable risk factor to reduce mortality in post-stroke population. *Neural regeneration research, 12*(3), 351-353.

15. Du, H., Cai, W., Xu, Y., Wang, Z., Wang, Y., & Cai, Y. (2017). Quantifying the cool island effects of urban green spaces using remote sensing Data. *Urban Forestry & Urban Greening, 27*, 24-31.

16. Elsayed, I. S. (2012). Mitigation of the urban heat island of the city of Kuala Lumpur, Malaysia. *Middle-East Journal of Scientific Research, 11*(11), 1602-1613.

17. EPA., (2014). Reducing Urban Heat Islands: Compendium of Strategies:Heat Island Reduction Activity.

18. Fisher, B. S., & Nasar, J. L. (1992). Fear of crime in relation to three exterior site features: Prospect, refuge, and escape. *Environment and behavior, 24*(1), 35-65.

19. Haaland, C., & van Den Bosch, C. K. (2015). Challenges and strategies for urban green-space planning in cities undergoing densification: A review. *Urban forestry & urban greening, 14*(4), 760-771

20. Haq, S. M. A. (2011). Urban green spaces and an integrative approach to sustainable environment. *Journal of environmental protection, 2*(5), 601-608.

21. Ibrahim, P. H. (2015). Masalah pengurusan kawasan lapang oleh pihak berkuasa tempatan di Malaysia. *IIUM Journal, 7, p 181, 182.*

22. Isa, N. A., Wan Mohd, W. M. N., & Salleh, S. A. (2017). The effects of built-up and green areas on the land surface temperature of the Kuala Lumpur City. *The International Archives of the Photogrammetry, Remote Sensing and Spatial Information Sciences, 42,* 107-112.

23. Jiang, J., & Tian, G. (2010). Analysis of the impact of land use/land cover change on land surface temperature with remote sensing. *Procedia environmental sciences, 2,* 571-575.

24. Jim, C. Y., & Chen, W. Y. (2006). Impacts of urban environmental elements on residential housing prices in Guangzhou (China). *Landscape and urban planning, 78*(4), 422-434.

25. Kabisch, N., Strohbach, M., Haase, D., & Kronenberg, J. (2016). Urban green space availability in European cities. *Ecological indicators, 70,* 586-596.

26. Kanniah, K. D. (2017). Quantifying green cover change for sustainable urban planning: A case of Kuala Lumpur, Malaysia. *Urban Forestry & Urban Greening, 27,* 287-304.

27. Kanniah, K.D., (2017). Change for Sustainable Urban Planning: A Case Of Kuala Lumpur, Malaysia.

28. Karuppannan, S., Baharuddin, Z. M., Sivam, A., & Daniels, C. B. (2014). Urban green space and urban biodiversity: Kuala Lumpur, Malaysia. *Journal of Sustainable Development, 7*(1), 1.

29. Kim, H., Lee, D. K., & Sung, S. (2016). Effect of urban green spaces and flooded area type on flooding probability. *Sustainability, 8*(2), 134.

30. Kim, J. P. (2009). *Land-use planning and the urban heat island effect.* The Ohio State University.

31. Kuo, F. E., & Sullivan, W. C. (2001). Environment and crime in the inner city: Does vegetation reduce crime?. *Environment and behavior, 33*(3), 343-367.

32. Kuo, F.E., & Sullivan, W.C., (2001). "Environment and Crime in The Inner City: Does Vegetation Reduce Crime?" *Environment and Behaviour, 33*(3), 343-367

33. Lee, A. C., & Maheswaran, R. (2011). The health benefits of urban green spaces: a review of the evidence. *Journal of public health, 33*(2), 212-222.

34. Lee, A.C.K., & Maheswaran, R.,(2017). The Health Benefits of Urban Green Spaces : A Review of The Evidence, *Journal of public health,* 33(2), 212–222.

35. Liu, H. L., & Shen, Y. S. (2014). The impact of green space changes on air pollution and microclimates: A case study of the Taipei metropolitan area. *Sustainability, 6*(12), 8827-8855.

36. Locke, D. H., Han, S., Kondo, M. C., Murphy-Dunning, C., & Cox, M. (2017). Did community greening reduce crime? Evidence from New Haven, CT, 1996–2007. *Landscape and Urban Planning, 161*, 72-79.

37. M'Ikiugu, M. M., Kinoshita, I., & Tashiro, Y. (2012). Urban green space analysis and identification of its potential expansion areas. *Procedia-Social and Behavioral Sciences, 35*, 449-458.

38. Manlun, Y. (2003, September). Suitability Analysis of Urban Green Space System Based on GIS. Geneva, Switzerland: ITC.

39. Mansor, M., & Harun, N. Z. (2014). Health issues and awareness, and the significant of green space for health promotion in Malaysia. *Procedia-Social and Behavioral Sciences, 153*, 209-220.

40. Mansor, M., & Said, I. (2008). Green infrastructure network as social spaces for well-being of residents in Taping, Malaysia. *Jurnal Alam Bina, 11*(2), 1-18.

41. Marzukhi, M. A., Karim, H. A., & Latfi, M. F. (2012). Evaluating the Shah Alam city council policy and guidelines on the hierarchy of neighborhood open space. *Procedia-Social and Behavioral Sciences, 36*, 456-465.

42. Mensah, C. A. (2014). Destruction of urban green spaces: A problem beyond urbanization in Kumasi city (Ghana). *American Journal of Environmental Protection, 3*(1), 1-9.

43. Michael, S. E., Hull, R. B., & Zahm, D. L. (2001). Environmental factors influencing auto burglary: A case study. *Environment and Behavior, 33*(3), 368-388.

44. Miller, J. R. (2005). Biodiversity conservation and the extinction of experience. *Trends in ecology & evolution,20*(8), 430-434.

45. Ministry of Natural Resources and Environment of Malaysia, (2016). National Policy on Biological and Diversity 2016-2025, Putrajaya.

46. Mohammadian, H., Tavakoli, J., Khani, H., (2017). Monitoring land use change and measuring urban sprawl based on its spatial forms The case of Qom city. *The Egyptian Journal of Remote Sensing and Space Sciences*, 20(1), 103–116.

47. Mohd Yusof, M.J., (2012). The True Colours of Urban Green Spaces: Identifying and Assessing the Qualities of Green Spaces in Kuala Lumpur, Malaysia. University of Edinburgh.

48. Mosammam, H. M., Nia, J. T., Khani, H., Teymouri, A., & Kazemi, M. (2017). Monitoring land use change and measuring urban sprawl based on its spatial forms: The case of Qom city. *The Egyptian Journal of Remote Sensing and Space Science, 20*(1), 103-116.

49. Myers, S. S., Gaffikin, L., Golden, C. D., Ostfeld, R. S., H. Redford, K., H. Ricketts, T., ... & Osofsky, S. A. (2013). Human health impacts of ecosystem alteration. *Proceedings of the National Academy of Sciences, 110*(47), 18753-18760.

50. Nor, A. N. M., Corstanje, R., Harris, J. A., & Brewer, T. (2017). Impact of rapid urban expansion on green space structure. *Ecological Indicators, 81*, 274-284.

51. NYC Economic Development Corporation., (2016).The High Line. Nezar Atta-Allah Kafafy., 2010. The dynamics of urban green space in an arid city; the case of Cairo- Egypt. Cardiff University.

52. Roberts, H. V. (2017). Using Twitter data in urban green space research: A case study and critical evaluation. *Applied Geography, 81*, 13-20.

53. Santos, T., Tenedório, J. A., & Gonçalves, J. A. (2016). Quantifying the city's green area potential gain using remote sensing data. *Sustainability, 8*(12), 1247.

54. Sorensen, M., Smit, J., & Barzetti, V. (1997). Good practices for urban greening.

55. Stigsdotter, U.K., (2014). Urban Green Spaces: Promoting Health Through City Planning, (November).

56. UN DESA., 2016. World Urbanisation Prospects.

57. Valipoor, N., & Dehkordi, K. S. (2016). Prioritizing Effective Factors on Liveliness and Improvement of the Urban Life Caused by the Development of Green Spaces with the Attraction- Repulsion Pattern. *Modern Applied Science, 10*(8), 90.

58. Van Herzele, A., & Wiedemann, T. (2003). A monitoring tool for the provision of accessible and attractive urban green spaces. *Landscape and urban planning, 63*(2), 109-126.

59. Waldner, L. S. (2009). Into the black hole: Do local governments implement their spatial policies?. *Land Use Policy, 26*(3), 818-827.

60. Wilson, J.Q. and Kelling, G., (1982). The police and neighborhood safety: broken windows. Atlantic Monthly, 127, 29–38.

61. World Health Organization., 2014. 7 million premature deaths annually linked to air pollution.

5. Innovative Approaches in Breast Cancer Diagnosis: Molecular Markers at The Forefront

Keshavamurthy M[1], Aastha[2], Manjula A.C*[3]

[1,2]Department of Life Sciences, Acharya Bangalore B-School, Bengaluru, Karnataka, India.

[3]Department of Sericulture, Maharani Cluster University, Maharani's Science College for Women, Bengaluru, Karnataka, India.

Author details & Affiliation

[1]Dr. Keshavamurthy M. Assistant Professor & Head, Department of Life Sciences, Acharya Bangalore B-School (Autonomous), Bengaluru – 560 091, Karnataka, India.

Email: *keshava.micro@gmail.com*

* Corresponding author:

[3]Dr. Manjula A. C., Professor, Department of Sericulture, Maharani Cluster University, Maharani's Science College for Women, Bengaluru - 560 001, Karnataka, India.

Email: dracmanjulam3@gmail.com

Abstract:

Breast cancer, a complex and heterogeneous disease, continues to pose significant challenges in diagnosis and treatment. This abstract provides a concise overview of the current state and recent advancements in the field of molecular markers and diagnostics for breast cancer. The chapter explores the diverse landscape of biomarkers, emphasizing their pivotal role in revolutionizing cancer detection, prognosis, and personalized therapeutic interventions. From established markers such as HER2/neu, estrogen receptor (ER), and progesterone receptor (PR) to emerging technologies like liquid biopsies and gene expression profiling, the chapter delves into the intricate molecular signatures that underlie breast cancer subtypes. The significance of molecular markers in early detection is highlighted, underscoring their potential to facilitate timely intervention and improve patient outcomes. Biomarkers not only aid in accurate diagnosis but also contribute to the ongoing efforts in cancer subtyping, enabling tailored treatment strategies. Moreover, the chapter explores the predictive and prognostic value of biomarkers, offering insights into treatment response and disease progression. In addition to their clinical applications, molecular markers play a crucial role in the era of personalized medicine, where treatment decisions are finely tuned to an individual's unique molecular profile. The integration of biomarker-based diagnostics minimizes invasiveness, offering less intrusive alternatives to traditional diagnostic procedures. The abstract also touches upon the challenges associated with current molecular diagnostics and envisions future directions in the field. As technology continues to advance, the chapter discusses the role of next-generation sequencing, artificial intelligence, and other cutting-edge methodologies in shaping the future of breast cancer diagnostics. This comprehensive overview, enriched with case studies and real-world applications, aims to provide a valuable resource for clinicians, researchers, and healthcare professionals seeking a deeper understanding of the evolving landscape of molecular markers and diagnostics in breast cancer. The insights presented herein contribute to the ongoing discourse in cancer research and guide the way towards more effective and personalized breast cancer management.

Keywords: Cancer, Molecular Markers, Diagnosis, Genomic Profiling, Imaging Advancements.

1. Introduction:

Breast cancer is heterogenous disease and one of the most frequent causes of death due to malignant neoplasms in women. In the past three decades, the incidence of this kind of cancer has more than doubled, with over 16,000 new cases recorded in 2010 (Walaszczyk & Gabryś, 2018). Despite significant strides in its diagnosis and treatment, challenges persist, necessitating ongoing research and innovation. Molecular markers and diagnostics have emerged as crucial tools in understanding breast cancer biology, enabling personalized therapeutic approaches and improving patient outcomes. Molecular markers, such as genetic mutations, gene expression profiles, and protein biomarkers, offer insights into tumour biology, prognosis, and treatment response (Inoue & Fry, 2016). Recent advances in genomic and transcriptome analysis have revealed the various molecular subtypes of breast cancer, which have implications for prognostic evaluations and therapy choices. Differentiating between luminal A, luminal B, HER2-enriched, basal-like, and normal-like subtypes has made it easier to develop customised treatment plans that include chemotherapy, hormone therapy, and HER2-targeted medications (Lang et al., 2015). Moreover, the discovery of particular genetic changes, such BRCA1 and BRCA2 mutations, has consequences for risk assessment and treatment choice, resulting in the creation of tailored medicines like PARP inhibitors for hereditary breast cancer.

2. Molecular Marker:

Molecular marker is a specific type of biomarker that can be a gene, transcript, or protein (or sets of such molecules) whose state and quantity are connected to the likelihood, occurrence, or progression of the illness(Al-Samarai & Al-Kazaz, 2015). A wide range of scientific fields, including genetics, genomics, plant and animal breeding, forensics, and medical diagnostics, are impacted by the significance of molecular markers. Molecular markers also give scientists the tools they need to investigate evolutionary processes, understand population dynamics, and track the genesis and spread of species (Dar et al., 2019). There are several types of molecular markers which can be sub-divided into three categories (Hasan et al., 2021). Three categories are distinguished among molecular markers according to the methods used for their detection. The first group consists of indicators for hybridization such as restriction fragment length polymorphism (RFLP), the second group consists of PCR-based markers like sequence-related amplified polymorphism (SRAP), inter-simple sequence repeats (ISSR), random amplified polymorphic DNA (RAPD), amplified fragment length polymorphism (AFLP), simple sequence repeats or microsatellites (SSR), sequence characterised amplified region (SCAR), and the third group includes DNA sequenced based molecular markers such as single nucleotide polymorphism (SNP), diverse array technology (DArT), and next generation sequencing (NGS).

3. Biomarkers in Breast Cancer:

Biomarkers refer to any quantifiable marker of a biological phenomenon, illness, or therapeutic reaction. Biomarkers are a broad class of properties that can be objectively measured and assessed as markers of pathogenic processes, normal biological processes, or pharmacological responses to therapeutic interventions (Gamble et al., 2021). However, there are two types of biomarkers related to treatment success and expected clinical outcomes in breast cancer subtypes, i.e., prognostic and predictive biomarkers (Fine & Pencina, 2015).

Followings are few of the classic biomarkers used in the diagnosis of breast cancer:

Ki-67: Ki-67 is a nucleolar nonhistone protein in human which is encoded by the MKI-67 gene, located on chromosome 10q26.2(Rakha et al., 2022). In breast cancer, it is related to cell proliferation and biological aggressiveness. Its prognostic value can predict survival and recurrence rates and can be used for primary tumour classification and metastases. Ki-67 is particularly useful in hormone receptor-positive cases as a discriminator between luminal A and B types. In neoadjuvant endocrine therapy (NET), Ki-67 measurement after short treatment reveals a biological response(Zhang et al., 2021).

However, due to doubts about its analytical validity, Ki-67 is not widely used in clinical routines due to variability in scoring methods and antibody reliability. Guidelines are needed for uniformity, standardization, and clinical validation.

Estrogen Receptor (ER): Estrogen receptor is a nuclear receptor that acts as a transcription factor, with two isoforms: ERα and ERβ. In breast cancer, ERα is the main form, affecting genes related to cell survival and proliferation whereas the role of ERβ is not well understood till now(Esteva & Hortobagyi, 2004). ER is a widely used predictive marker in breast cancer diagnosis and treatment using endocrine therapy (ET). ER measurement is mandatory in newly diagnosed cases, and ER expression is recognized as a biomarker of favourable prognosis. Response to ET depends on ER positivity and varies according to ER tumour expression levels (Mills et al., 2018). Estrogen suppression treatments use ER antagonists to kill ER-positive BC cells. Several ETs are approved for adjuvant treatment of ER-positive BC patients, improving survival and time to disease recurrence. In luminal-type BC, adjuvant ET is standard and recommended for at least 5 years after surgery.ETs include aromatase inhibitors (AIs), selective estrogen receptor modulators (SERMs), and selective estrogen receptor degraders (SERDs). AIs block estrogen biosynthesis, while SRMs compete with estrogen for ER binding and may have antagonistic activity in breast tissue. SRDs have ER degrading and antagonistic effects and anti-estrogenic effects(Brufsky & Dickler, 2018).

ET resistance can influence therapy results, with the most common case being estrogen-independent ER reactivation due to specific ESR1 gene mutations(Brett et al., 2021). Acquired resistance can be circumvented by using other classes of ET, which can be used sequentially to treat ER-positive cases. Some ET treatments target other molecules, such as CDK4/6, PI3K, or mTORC1.

Progesterone Receptor (PR): The progesterone receptor (PR) is a member of nuclear receptor family that acts as ligand-activated transcription factors and binds to the DNA in its active form which regulates cell cycle genes, cell differentiation, and proliferation. It is typically measured alongside estrogen (ER) in newly diagnosed cases and recurrent and metastatic lesions (Cenciarini & Proietti, 2019). PR is a biomarker that indicates a functional and intact ER pathway, which directly impacts a tumor's ability to respond to endocrine therapies (ETs). PR positivity also shows a better response to ETs, and PR-positive tumor patients generally have better clinical outcomes. High PR expression may be related to a better tamoxifen response, lower recurrence rate, and longer disease-free survival.

Semi-quantitative PR scores, obtained through tests like PAM50, help discriminate BC types, such as luminal A and B. High PR expression is observed more commonly in Luminal A subtypes, which show better prognosis than Luminal B(Li et al., 2022). Studies have shown that PR can associate with ERα, modulating its expression and directing its binding to chromatin. Selective progesterone receptor modulators (SPRMs) are being studied in clinical trials to modulate and induce agonist, antagonist, or mixed PR responses in a tissue-specific manner. Mifepristone, telapristone acetate, and onapristone are antiprogestogens that have had positive responses in patients who did not respond to other treatments.

4. Human Epidermal Growth Factor Receptor 2:

HER2 (human epidermal growth factor receptor 2) is a member of the human epidermal growth factor receptor family, and its overexpression in breast cancer (BC) is associated with a worse prognosis due to the high metastatic potential of HER2-positive tumors(Kunte et al., 2020). HER2 status is determined by immunohistochemistry (IHC) and/or in situ hybridization (ISH). HER2 activation occurs through dimerization after ligand binding, and its signaling leads to tumor growth, proliferation, adhesion, cell survival, and metastasis. Overexpression leads to aggressive histological characteristics and a shorter survival time.

HER2 status measurement is mandatory in cases of invasive BC and recommended in cases of recurrence and metastasis. Anti-HER-2 targeting therapies have shown efficacy in BC cases marked by ERBB2 amplification or the overexpression of the HER protein(Wynn & Tang, 2022). These therapies currently involve the use of drugs based on anti-HER2 monoclonal antibodies, tyrosine kinase inhibitors (TKIS), and antibody-drug conjugates (ADCs). Initial therapy for metastatic HER-2 tumors uses a combination of two HER2 antibodies, pertuzumab and trastuzumab, associated with a taxane.

Intra- and intertumoral HER2 heterogeneity negatively affects the response to anti-HER2 therapy, leading to shorter recurrence time and patient survival, increased tumor size, worse histology, and greater number of lymph node metastases. Change in HER2 status after metastasis affects therapeutic strategies, with tumor resistance in metastatic tumors more frequent. TKIs have a smaller size and greater penetration capacity, making lapatinib, tucatinib, and neratinib a better option for patients with brain metastases.

5. Genetic Basis: BRCA1 and BRCA2 Mutations:

BRCA1 and BRCA2 genes are the two most common in autosomal dominant and high penetrance forms of breast and ovarian cancer. They produce Tumor Suppressor Gene (TSG) proteins, making them TSGs. BRCA1 is located on chr17q, and any changes or mutations in this gene can increase the risk of developing breast, ovarian, and prostate cancer. BRCA2 is located on chr13q, an acrocentric chromosome in men, and any mutations can increase the risk of developing these cancers.

Two genes, BRCA1 and BRCA2, are responsible for cell growth suppressors and producing TSG proteins. BRCA1 has 1863 amino acids and has been the site of 300 disease-causing mutations. BRCA2 has 3418 amino acids and is also called an anti-oncogene. If either gene is damaged, damaged DNA will not be repaired, leading to more changes and mutations in cell DNA, ultimately leading to cancer(Mehrgou & Akouchekian, 2016). The Loss of Heterozygosity (LOH) phenomenon can occur in these genes, leading to another healthy allele mutated. This can impair TSG performance, making cells more susceptible to tumor development and cancer. The BRCA2 gene is the second breast cancer predisposing gene, crucial for intact double-strand DNA break repair and transcription regulation. Mutations in BRCA1 can cause 60% to 80% breast cancer in women, an increased risk of ovarian cancer in women and prostate cancer in men. BRCA2 germ-line mutations are found in approximately 35% of families with early-onset breast cancer in women and an increased risk of ovarian cancer in women and breast cancer in men.

BRCA1 gene mutations can cause breast cancer in women, increasing the risk of ovarian cancer and prostate cancer in men. Germ-line mutations in the BRCA2 gene are found in 35% of families with early-onset breast cancer in women and increase the risk of ovarian cancer development in women and breast cancer in men. BRCA1-related breast cancer has a higher incidence, higher mitotic rate, and more lymphatic penetration than sporadic breast cancer. Mutants are more likely to lack expression of ER, PR, and HER-2nue receptors and have a somatic mutation in the P53 gene. Mutation carriers also have an increased risk for other cancers like colon, prostate, pancreatic, melanoma, and gastric cancers. Novel mutations in BRCA1 and BRCA2 genes are rare, with 2000 mutations discovered so far. Most breast cancer-causing mutations in BRCA1 and BRCA2 genes lead to producing truncated protein through nonsense, frame shift, and splicing mutaciones (Abu-Helalah et al., 2020).

However, there are some non-BRCA genes which is rare, so routine genetic testing isn't widely used. In the future, testing for genetic susceptibility will involve panels of genes or whole-exome sequencing, saving time and costs. However, interpretation of results is complicated due to lack of data and unclear clinical significance. Table 1 lists other genes linked to increased breast cancer susceptibility.

Table 1: Breast Cancer Susceptibility Genes and their Penetrance (Frey et al., 2017).

GENE	PENETRANCE
BRCA1/2	High
TP53	High
LKB1	High
CHEK2	Moderate
ATM	Moderate
PALB	Moderate

6. Gene Expression Profiling:

Gene expression profiling is a method that uses genetic microarrays to analyze genetic transcriptional variations between normal and malignant cells. It identifies the expression levels of thousands of genes in breast cancer and provides molecular profiles. Originally developed in the mid-1990s, it focuses on the transcription of messenger RNAs (mRNA) into proteins, which in turn affect cell characteristics and functions. This method uses complementary DNA (cDNA) or oligonucleotide microarrays to probe gene expression in mRNA extracted from frozen or paraffin-fixed tissue (Bao & Davidson, 2008). Tests that look at various sets of breast cancer genes to determine whether chemotherapy is necessary to help lower the risk of cancer returning (recurrence) include Oncotype DX, MammaPrint, and Endopredict. There are now more tests being developed. The test type that is administered will vary based on patient's circumstances.

Table 2: Gene Expression Tests for Predicting Clinical Outcomes in Patients with HR positive, HER2 negative, Node 0-3 Positive Early-stage Breast Cancer

	Oncotype DX	MammaPrint	EndoPrint
Manufacturer	Genomic health	Agendia	Myriad Genetics
Tissue Sample	FFPE	Fresh, frozen, or FFPE	FFPE
No. Of genes	16 cancer 5 control	70	8 cancer

Technology	Quantitative RT-PCR	Microarrays	Quantitative-RT-PCR
Predictive	+	-	-
Prognostic	+	+	+
Eligible patients	ER+ andHER2-,T1/2 0-3 nodes	Stage I and II breast cancer	ER+ HER2-
Measure/ categories	RS Low<18 Intermediate 18-31 High >31	Good risk and poor risk intrinsic subtype	The test result is composed of the 'molecular fingerprint' of a tumor
Strength of ASCO recommendation	Strong for N0 Moderate for N+	Moderate for N0 and N+	Moderate for N0 and N+
8th AJCC breast cancer staging manual (when available as stage modifiers).	For patients with HR+, HER-, and ALN- tumors, Oncotype DX recurrence score less than 11, regardless of T size, places the tumor in the same prognostic category	For the patients with HR+, HER-, and ALN- tumors, PAM50 ROR score in the low-range, regardless of T-size, places the tumor in the same prognostic category	For the patients with HR+, HER-, and ALN- tumors, Endopredict low-risk score, regardless of T size, places the tumor in the same prognostic category

(Source: Malvia et al., 2019)

ALN: axillary lymph node; ASCO: American Society of Clinical Oncology; FFPE: formaline-fixed parafine embedded; RT-PCR: reverse transcriptase-polymerase chain reaction; ER: estrogen receptor; HR: hormone receptor.

7. Conclusion:

The integration of molecular markers marks a revolutionary leap forward in breast cancer diagnosis. Through these pioneering methods, healthcare providers can attain earlier detection, precise prognosis, and tailor-made treatment plans. This transformative change not only enhances patient outcomes but also emphasizes the essential role of molecular markers in shaping the future of breast cancer care. As ongoing research progresses, these technologies hold the potential to continuously enhance our comprehension and treatment of this intricate disease, fostering optimism for enhanced survival rates and better quality of life globally.

References:

1. Abu-Helalah, M., Azab, B., Mubaidin, R., Ali, D., Jafar, H., Alshraideh, H., Drou, N., & Awidi, A. (2020). BRCA1 and BRCA2 genes mutations among high risk breast cancer patients in Jordan. *Scientific Reports*, *10*(1). https://doi.org/10.1038/s41598-020-74250-2

2. Al-Samarai, F. R., & Al-Kazaz, A. A. (2015). Molecular Markers: an Introduction and Applications. *European Journal of Molecular Biotechnology*, *9*(3), 118–130. https://doi.org/10.13187/ejmb.2015.9.118

3. Bao, T., & Davidson, N. E. (2008). Gene Expression Profiling of Breast Cancer. In *Advances in Surgery* (Vol. 42, Issue C, pp. 249–260). https://doi.org/10.1016/j.yasu.2008.03.002

4. Brett, J. O., Spring, L. M., Bardia, A., & Wander, S. A. (2021). ESR1 mutation as an emerging clinical biomarker in metastatic hormone receptor-positive breast cancer. In *Breast Cancer Research* (Vol. 23, Issue 1). BioMed Central Ltd. https://doi.org/10.1186/s13058-021-01462-3 *brody1998*. (n.d.).

5. Brufsky, A. M., & Dickler, M. N. (2018). Estrogen Receptor-Positive Breast Cancer: Exploiting Signaling Pathways Implicated in Endocrine Resistance. *The Oncologist*, *23*(5), 528–539. https://doi.org/10.1634/theoncologist.2017-0423

6. Cenciarini, M. E., & Proietti, C. J. (2019). Molecular mechanisms underlying progesterone receptor action in breast cancer: Insights into cell proliferation and stem cell regulation. *Steroids*, *152*. https://doi.org/10.1016/j.steroids.2019.108503

7. Dar, A. A., Mahajan, R., & Sharma, S. (2019). Molecular markers for characterization and conservation of plant genetic resources. *Indian Journal of Agricultural Sciences*, *89*(11), 1755–1763. https://doi.org/10.56093/ijas.v89i11.95286

8. Esteva, F. J., & Hortobagyi, G. N. (2004). Prognostic molecular markers in early breast cancer. In *Breast Cancer Research* (Vol. 6, Issue 3, pp. 109–118). https://doi.org/10.1186/bcr777

9.   Fine, J. P., & Pencina, M. J. (2015). On the Quantitative Assessment of Predictive Biomarkers. In *Journal of the National Cancer Institute* (Vol. 107, Issue 8). Oxford University Press. https://doi.org/10.1093/jnci/djv187

10.   Frey, J. D., Salibian, A. A., Schnabel, F. R., Choi, M., & Karp, N. S. (2017). Non-BRCA1/2 Breast Cancer Susceptibility Genes: A New Frontier with Clinical Consequences for Plastic Surgeons. *Plastic and Reconstructive Surgery - Global Open*, 5(11). https://doi.org/10.1097/GOX.0000000000001564

11.   Gamble, P., Jaroensri, R., Wang, H., Tan, F., Moran, M., Brown, T., Flament-Auvigne, I., Rakha, E. A., Toss, M., Dabbs, D. J., Regitnig, P., Olson, N., Wren, J. H., Robinson, C., Corrado, G. S., Peng, L. H., Liu, Y., Mermel, C. H., Steiner, D. F., & Chen, P.-H. C. (2021). Determining breast cancer biomarker status and associated morphological features using deep learning. *Communications Medicine*, 1(1). https://doi.org/10.1038/s43856-021-00013-3

12.   Hasan, N., Choudhary, S., Naaz, N., Sharma, N., & Laskar, R. A. (2021). Recent advancements in molecular marker-assisted selection and applications in plant breeding programmes. In *Journal of Genetic Engineering and Biotechnology* (Vol. 19, Issue 1). Springer Science and Business Media Deutschland GmbH. https://doi.org/10.1186/s43141-021-00231-1

13.   Inoue, K., & Fry, E. A. (2016). Novel Molecular Markers for Breast Cancer. *Biomarkers in Cancer*, 8, BIC.S38394. https://doi.org/10.4137/BIC.S38394

14.   Kunte, S., Abraham, J., & Montero, A. J. (2020). Novel HER2–targeted therapies for HER2–positive metastatic breast cancer. In *Cancer* (Vol. 126, Issue 19, pp. 4278–4288). John Wiley and Sons Inc. https://doi.org/10.1002/cncr.33102

15.   Lang, J. E., Wecsler, J. S., Press, M. F., & Tripathy, D. (2015). Molecular markers for breast cancer diagnosis, prognosis and targeted therapy. *Journal of Surgical Oncology*, 111(1), 81–90. https://doi.org/10.1002/jso.23732

16.   Li, Z., Wei, H., Li, S., Wu, P., & Mao, X. (2022). The Role of Progesterone Receptors in Breast Cancer. In *Drug Design, Development and Therapy* (Vol. 16, pp. 305–314). Dove Medical Press Ltd. https://doi.org/10.2147/DDDT.S336643

17.   Malvia, S., Bagadi, S. A. R., Pradhan, D., Chintamani, C., Bhatnagar, A., Arora, D., Sarin, R., & Saxena, S. (2019). Study of Gene Expression Profiles of Breast Cancers in Indian Women. *Scientific Reports*, 9(1). https://doi.org/10.1038/s41598-019-46261-1

18. Mehrgou, A., & Akouchekian, M. (2016). The importance of BRCA1 and BRCA2 genes mutations in breast cancer development. In *Med J Islam Repub Iran* (Vol. 30, Issue 15). http://mjiri.iums.ac.ir

19. Mills, J. N., Rutkovsky, A. C., & Giordano, A. (2018). Mechanisms of resistance in estrogen receptor positive breast cancer: overcoming resistance to tamoxifen/aromatase inhibitors. In *Current Opinion in Pharmacology* (Vol. 41, pp. 59–65). Elsevier Ltd. https://doi.org/10.1016/j.coph.2018.04.009

20. Rakha, E. A., Chmielik, E., Schmitt, F. C., Tan, P. H., Quinn, C. M., & Gallagy, G. (2022). Assessment of Predictive Biomarkers in Breast Cancer: Challenges and Updates. In *Pathobiology* (Vol. 89, Issue 5, pp. 263–277). S. Karger AG. https://doi.org/10.1159/000525092

21. Scope, A., Essat, M., Pandor, A., Rafia, R., Ward, S. E., Wyld, L., Cross, S., & Woods, H. B. (2017). Gene expression profiling and expanded immunohistochemistry tests to guide selection of chemotherapy regimens in breast cancer management: A systematic review. In *International Journal of Technology Assessment in Health Care* (Vol. 33, Issue 1, pp. 32–45). Cambridge University Press. https://doi.org/10.1017/S0266462317000034

22. Sotiriou, C., Wirapati, P., Loi, S., Harris, A., Fox, S., Smeds, J., Nordgren, H., Farmer, P., Praz, V., Haibe-Kains, B., Desmedt, C., Larsimont, D., Cardoso, F., Peterse, H., Nuyten, D., Buyse, M., Van de Vijver, M. J., Bergh, J., Piccart, M., & Delorenzi, M. (2006). Gene expression profiling in breast cancer: Understanding the molecular basis of histologic grade to improve prognosis. *Journal of the National Cancer Institute, 98*(4), 262–272. https://doi.org/10.1093/jnci/djj052

23. Van't Veer, L. J., Paik, S., & Hayes, D. F. (2005). Gene expression profiling of breast cancer: A new tumor marker. In *Journal of Clinical Oncology* (Vol. 23, Issue 8, pp. 1631–1635). https://doi.org/10.1200/JCO.2005.12.005

24. Walaszczyk, A., & Gabryś, D. (2018). Molecular markers used in breast cancer diagnosis — Current practice and future perspectives. In *Nowotwory* (Vol. 68, Issues 5–6, pp. 259–267). Via Medica. https://doi.org/10.5603/NJO.2018.0041

25. Wynn, C. S., & Tang, S. C. (2022). Anti-HER2 therapy in metastatic breast cancer: many choices and future directions. In *Cancer and Metastasis Reviews* (Vol. 41, Issue 1, pp. 193–209). Springer. https://doi.org/10.1007/s10555-022-10021-x

26. Zambelli, A., Tondini, C., Munkácsy, G., Santarpia, L., Gy, B., & Orffy, ". (2022). *Gene Expression Profiling in Early Breast Cancer-Patient Stratification Based on Molecular and Tumor Microenvironment Features.* https://doi.org/10.3390/biomedicines

27. Zhang, A., Wang, X., Fan, C., & Mao, X. (2021). The Role of Ki67 in Evaluating Neoadjuvant Endocrine Therapy of Hormone Receptor-Positive Breast Cancer. In *Frontiers in Endocrinology* (Vol. 12). Frontiers Media S.A. https://doi.org/10.3389/fendo.2021.687244

6. Role of International Law in Environment Protection

Mr. Vikant Kumar and Ms. Prachi Tyagi

Assistant Professor, Vivek college of Law, Bijnor

Email: vikantku007@gmail.com

Email: tyagiprachi666@gmail.com

Abstract:

Environmental issues require an international response since they go beyond national boundaries. As a crucial foundation for this reaction, international environmental law (IEL) has arisen, encouraging collaboration and imposing legal duties on nations to safeguard the environment. The many facets of IEL's contribution in protecting the environment are examined in this abstract. First, IEL uses treaties and accords to create a shared understanding of environmental risks. A sense of shared responsibility is fostered by platforms such as the United Nations Environment Programme (UNEP), which allow knowledge sharing and risk assessment. These agreements put this comprehension into practice. One example of effective international collaboration in combating ozone depletion is the Montreal Protocol. IEL promotes technology transfer and knowledge sharing in addition to treaties. Developed countries may help developing countries address environmental challenges more successfully by imparting to them their knowledge in fields like renewable energy. In addition, IEL encourages the development of funding for environmental initiatives in poor countries, assisting with initiatives like biodiversity preservation, deforestation avoidance, and climate change adaptation. Education and public awareness campaigns are essential components of environmental conservation. Collaboration among nations promotes changes in the world's habits towards sustainability. International organizations and non-governmental organizations work together to increase public awareness of environmental concerns and promote ethical conduct, enabling people to take an active role in environmental conservation.

Keywords: Environment, International Law, Environment Protection, sustainable development, Education.

1. Introduction:

Environmental issues transcend national boundaries. Environmental problems need an international response, from migrating birds transporting pollution to increasing sea levels endangering coasts everywhere (Ong, 2010). This is the point where global collaboration becomes paramount, essential to preserving our world. Environmental protection was traditionally seen as a national issue. But as the globe grew more interconnected and the transboundary character of environmental issues became apparent, a change was required. The basis for coordinated action that arose is international environmental law. This legal framework consists of treaties, conventions, and agreements that impose responsibilities on member nations and specify environmental goals. The development of a shared knowledge of environmental risks is one of the most important results of international collaboration. Nations come together through platforms such as the United Nations Environment Programme (UNEP) to exchange knowledge, evaluate environmental hazards, and devise remedies. This cooperative strategy motivates nations to put the welfare of the planet ahead of their own interests by fostering a feeling of shared responsibility (Ivanova, 2010). This understanding is put into practice by international accords. One example of effective international collaboration in combating ozone depletion is the Montreal Protocol. Through the gradual elimination of hazardous substances, this agreement preserved the ozone layer, shielding humans from heightened UV rays. In a similar vein, the Paris Climate Agreement signifies a worldwide commitment to cutting greenhouse gas emissions and lessening the effects of climate change. International collaboration transcends legal structures. It encourages the sharing of cutting-edge techniques and tools. Developed countries may impart to poor countries their knowledge in fields such as sustainable waste management and renewable energy. Countries are better equipped to handle environmental issues as a result of this knowledge transfer. Another essential component of global environmental conservation is financial resources. Funds supporting environmental projects in underdeveloped countries are frequently contributed to by developed countries. Initiatives like stopping deforestation, protecting biodiversity, and preparing for climate change can be funded with the help of these funding. Promoting environmental education and awareness also heavily depends on international collaboration. International organizations and non-governmental organizations (NGOs) working together can promote a worldwide transition to sustainable practices. Through increasing environmental awareness and promoting conscientious conduct, global collaboration enables people to take an active role in safeguarding the environment. But there are obstacles in the way of environmental conservation on a global scale. International agreements may be difficult to negotiate and implement because they frequently call for compromise between countries with different goals and economic realities. Furthermore, strong monitoring and enforcement systems are needed to guarantee adherence to these agreements. International collaboration continues to be the cornerstone of successful environmental preservation in spite of these obstacles. The best chance for a sustainable future in a world where environmental dangers are interrelated is via concerted action. The international community can guarantee a healthy world for future generations by encouraging cooperation, information exchange, and resource allocation.

2. Acknowledgment:

At the end of the journey of this paper research project, from the beginning until the date of completion, we have come across several people, a variety of experiences, and a lot of effort. Today, We would like to mention all those who have been, directly or indirectly, of great support to us and our work. We would like to express our gratitude, especially to our friends and colleagues who, having been experienced in the field, helped us to understand the concept and its relevance. We would like to thank our family. Without their adoration and assistance, we are nothing. Our Parent's blessings are something we owe them. The Cooperation and direction of our parents enabled us to get an education of this level, and their blessings inspired us to complete this work.

3. Objectives:
- The following are the study's objectives:
- To study international laws on Environment protection.
- To study the impact of international law on environment protection.

4. Hypothesis:

This research has been conducted with a view to testing the hypothesis formulated as follows: The International Law in all over the world plays a significant role in protection of environment.

5. Statement of Problem:

The global endeavor to protect our environment confronts a severe predicament. Global unity is required to address environmental dangers such as ocean acidification and climate change, which transcend state boundaries. A foundation for collaboration is provided by international environmental legislation, with agreements like the Paris Agreement establishing challenging objectives. Enforcement is still a major obstacle, though. Strong, coordinated action may be hampered by conflict between national interests and disparate economic realities. While poor countries could put short-term economic growth ahead of long-term environmental sustainability, developed nations might be reluctant to commit to rigorous restrictions that could have an impact on their economies. Furthermore, in a complex and constantly changing global environment, maintaining compliance with international accords needs strong monitoring and enforcement procedures, which can be difficult. The international community must close the gap between words and deeds in order to tackle these challenges by encouraging more cooperation, information exchange, and fair resource distribution. Future generations can only be properly protected from our planet if we work together in cooperation.

In order to protect the environment, In the field of environment protection, various treaties and conferences have been established effectively on international level by various countries to avoid clashes between nature and the environment. In this research, we will see the various conventions and conferences on international level, which plays significant role for the protection of environment. Along with it, we will see what the views of the various international courts are and how effective impact is there.

6. Declaration of Interest Statement:

There is no conflict of interest as per the financial statement, and the manuscript has been published only for academic purposes.

7. UDHR's Provisions Regarding Environment Protection:

Although there isn't an explicit clause addressing environmental preservation in the 1948 Universal Declaration of Human Rights (UDHR), it establishes the foundation for the idea through a series of interrelated rights and concepts. We will have a look at how the UDHR indirectly supports environmental protection:

To understand the various provisions of UDHR regarding environmental protection we can classified this in some categories as follows:

I. **Interdependence of Human Rights:** The universality and indivisibility of human rights are emphasized in the UDHR. This implies that the exercise of one right is frequently dependent upon the exercise of another. Many of the fundamental human rights stated in the declaration depend on a healthy environment. These includes:

- **Right to Life (Article 3):** A healthy environment, free from pollution and environmental degradation, is essential for sustaining life.
- **Right to Health (Article 25):** Environmental factors like clean air, water, and sanitation significantly impact human health.

- **Right to an Adequate Standard of Living (Article 25):** This includes access to food, water, and shelter, all of which are directly affected by environmental conditions.
- **Right to Food (Article 25):** A healthy environment is crucial for sustainable food production and food security.
- **Right to Water and Sanitation (Article 25):** Access to clean water and sanitation is directly linked to environmental quality.

II. Sustainable Development: Although the idea of "sustainable development" was not commonly known in 1948, it was established by the UDHR principles (Acheampong, 2017). The social and economic rights included in Articles 22 through 27 emphasize the need for growth that satisfies current demands without jeopardizing the ability of future generations to satiate their own. A key component of sustainable development is environmental conservation, which makes sure that progress doesn't come at the expense of environmental deterioration that jeopardizes the welfare of future generations.

III. Evolving Landscape of Human Rights Law: After the UDHR was ratified, international human rights legislation has continued to develop. An important step was taken in 2022 by the UN General Assembly in consideration of the mounting environmental issues. It acknowledged as a human right the right to a hygienic, livable, and sustainable environment. This resolution represents a worldwide agreement on the significance of environmental preservation for human well-being, even if it is not legally enforceable.

8. Development of International Environmental Law:

International environmental law (IEL) is a relatively young field, but it has grown rapidly in response to pressing global challenges. Here's a look at its development:

- ➢ **Pre-1972: Stirrings of Awareness:**
  - Limited international cooperation on environmental issues existed before the 1970s.
  - Early efforts focused on specific concerns, like wildlife conservation (e.g., failed London Convention of 1900 for African wildlife protection).

- ➢ **1972: A Watershed Moment:**

A watershed was reached during the United Nations Conference on the Human Environment in Stockholm. It made the United Nations Environment Programme (UNEP) the focal point for matters pertaining to the environment. The conference's **Stockholm Declaration** laid the groundwork for IEL with 26 principles, including:

- State responsibility for transboundary environmental harm.
- The need for sustainable development.
- The right to a healthy environment (though not yet explicitly recognized).

➤ **Post -Stockholm: A Period of Growth:**

The 1970s and 1980s saw a surge in international environmental agreements:

- **Convention on International Trade in Endangered Species (CITES, 1973):** Regulates trade in endangered wildlife.
- **Vienna Convention for the Protection of the Ozone Layer (1985):** Framework for ozone layer protection.
- **Montreal Protocol (1987):** Phases out ozone-depleting substances (a landmark success story).
- **Basel Convention on the Control of Transboundary Movements of Hazardous Wastes and Their Disposal (1989):** Promotes safe management of hazardous waste.

➤ **1992: Rio Earth summit and beyond**

- The **United Nations Conference on Environment and Development (UNCED),** also known as the Rio Earth Summit, built upon the foundation laid in Stockholm.
- Key agreements were adopted:

    I. **Convention on Biological Diversity (CBD, 1992):** Promotes conservation and sustainable use of biodiversity.

    II. **Framework Convention on Climate Change (UNFCCC, 1992):** Tackles climate change through international cooperation.

    III. **Rio Declaration on Environment and Development:** Established principles for sustainable development.

Conferences the World Summit on Sustainable Development (2002) and like Rio+20 (2012) examined developments and new issues.

➤ **Recent Developments:**

- The **Paris Agreement (2015):** A landmark agreement under the UNFCCC, aiming to limit global warming to well below 2 degrees Celsius, preferably to 1.5 degrees Celsius.

- **Recognition of the right to a clean, healthy, and sustainable environment:** By the UN General Assembly in 2022, though not yet legally binding.

9. Judicial Decisions:

- The *Trail Smelter Arbitration Case,1941* between the United States and Canada, involved air pollution from a smelter in Canada harming vegetation in the US. While not specifically an environmental pact, it did create the sic utere tuo ut alienum non laedas concept ("so use your own property as not to injure that of another"). This idea has impacted environmental laws that have come after it.

- *This Lac Lanoux Arbitration (France v. Spain) (1957)* case, France and Spain shared a river, and there was disagreement about how to divide the available water supplies. It also laid the groundwork for another cornerstone of international environmental law: the equitable usage of common resources.

- In the *North Sea Continental Shelf Cases (1969),* the International court of Justice Although not specifically environmental, established guidelines for the fair distribution of resources are pertinent to issues involving the environment.

- In the Gabčíkovo-Nagymaros Project (Hungary v. Slovakia) (1997) case, there was Dispute over a dam project on the Danube River with potential environmental impacts .International Court of Justice balanced environmental concerns with treaty obligations and economic development.

- In the MOX Plant Case (Ireland v. United Kingdom) (2001) case, Ireland objected to the UK's nuclear fuel reprocessing because it would pose environmental hazards. The International court of justice emphasized the "precautionary principle" in environmental decision-making and reiterated the requirement to do environmental impact assessments.

- In The Pulp Mills on the River Uruguay (Argentina v. Uruguay) (2006) case, disagreement over the building of pulp mills on a shared river, which has led to worries about contamination of the water supply. The International court stressed that in order to prevent transboundary environmental impact, notification, consultation, and collaboration are crucial.

- In The Territorial Dispute (Guyana v. Suriname) (2007) case, The court recognized the value of safeguarding environmentally vulnerable places during border conflicts, even if its focus was not exclusively environmental.

- This Oleochemicals Plant Arbitration (Malaysia v. Singapore) (2008) case, addressed air pollution from an industrial plant in Malaysia impacting Singapore. It emphasized the obligation to prevent transboundary harm and the polluter pays principle.
- In The Indus Waters Kishenganga Arbitration (India v. Pakistan) (2013) case, Permanent court of Arbitration highlighted the importance of environmental impact assessments and information exchange in shared watercourse projects.

10. Conclusion:

In the last fifty years, there has been a significant shift in the field of international environmental law, or IEL. IEL has developed into a vital instrument for tackling environmental challenges on a worldwide scale, from its early phases prior to the 1970s to the acknowledgment of the right to a healthy environment in 2022. Nonetheless, there have been obstacles as well as advancements along the way. The Stockholm Conference in 1972 is considered a turning point. It made environmental issues more widely known and positioned UNEP as the leading authority on environmental issues. The ideas of sustainable development and state responsibility for transboundary environmental degradation lay the foundation for IEL in the Stockholm Declaration.

There was an explosion of international environmental accords in the next decades. Significant environmental challenges were addressed and foundations for international collaboration were formed by landmark treaties including the Framework Convention on Climate Change, the Convention on Biological Diversity, and the Montreal Protocol. These accords signaled a dramatic change in the direction of environmental protection—from dispersed, issue-specific measures to a more comprehensive and integrated approach. The commitment to sustainable development was further cemented during the Rio Earth Summit in 1992. It promoted cooperation between corporations, governments, and non-governmental organizations (NGOs), emphasizing the necessity of socially and ecologically responsible economic development. Conferences like Rio+20 and Stockholm+50 in 2022 have evaluated the state of the art and tackled new issues.

One notable and recent achievement is the Paris Agreement. Its audacious objective of reducing global warming is a concerted worldwide endeavor to address the most urgent environmental issue of our time. Furthermore, the UN General Assembly's 2022 acknowledgment of the right to a clean, healthy, and sustainable environment represents a significant advancement in the integration of environmental protection into the larger framework of human rights. IEL still faces difficulties in spite of these developments. International agreements may have complicated enforcement procedures, raising questions regarding their practical use. It is still difficult to strike a balance between economic development and environmental conservation, especially for developing countries. Novel legal solutions and continuous attention are needed for emerging concerns like biodiversity loss and climate change adaptation. A diverse strategy is needed to move towards a sustainable future. IEL offers a strong basis with its dynamic ideas and cooperative structure. But in order to guarantee that IEL continues to be an effective instrument for preserving our world for future generations, sustained dedication, creativity, and efficient execution are required. In order to ensure a healthy world for everybody, a strong and dynamic IEL framework will be essential as we confront a future filled with complex environmental concerns.

References:

1. Kothari, A. (2000). "India's Forests: Will Money Save Them".
2. Acheampong, K. A. (2017). Sustainable Development Goals, Stateless Individuals and Inclusive Education. *U. Botswana LJ*, *25*, 30.
3. Alexandre C. Kiss and Dinah, Shelton's. (2007) Guide to International Environmental Law
4. Allan Robert, (1980), How to Save the World Strategy for World Conservation, Kogan page, UNEP
5. Commission on Environment and Development (1987), Our Common Future, Oxford University Press
6. Ivanova, M. (2010). UNEP in global environmental governance: design, leadership, location. *Global Environmental Politics*, *10*(1), 30-59.
7. Jose George, (1984), Development and Environmental Hazards, Law and Environment, 1984, p-224-278
8. Ong, D. M. (2010). International environmental law governing threats to biological diversity. In *Research handbook on international environmental law*. Edward Elgar Publishing.
9. The Hindu Survey of Environment 2000. A. Kothari (2004). "Displacement Fears". Frontline. December 31, 2004.
10. United Nations Conference on Environment and Development (UNCED), 1992 ('Earth Summit'/'Rio Conference').

7. Traditional Practices of Environmental Conservation and Management in the Thar Desert of Rajasthan: A Historical Perspective

Jaspreet Singh

Department of History, Maharaja Ganga Singh University, Bikaner

Email: jaspreet1776@gmail.com

Abstract:

The Thar Desert of Rajasthan is a unique and fragile ecosystem that has sustained human life for centuries through the application of traditional ecological knowledge and practices. This study explores the historical development and contemporary relevance of these traditional methods in conserving and managing natural resources in the region. It examines how local communities have adapted to the harsh environmental conditions of the desert through innovative practices such as water harvesting, soil conservation, and agroforestry. The research highlights the cultural, social, and spiritual values embedded in these practices, demonstrating their integral role in fostering environmental sustainability and resilience. By documenting and analyzing these traditional practices, this study aims to inform modern conservation strategies and policy frameworks, emphasizing the importance of integrating indigenous knowledge with contemporary scientific approaches. The findings underscore the need for inclusive and context-specific interventions that respect and leverage the wisdom of local communities in addressing the environmental challenges of arid regions.

Keywords: Rajasthan, Thar Desert. Environment, Conservation, Biodiversity

1. Introduction:

The Thar Desert, also known as the Great Indian Desert, spans approximately 200,000 square kilometers, making it the 17th largest desert in the world and the 9th largest subtropical desert (Varghese, 2023). It covers a significant portion of Rajasthan and extends into the states of Gujarat, Punjab, and Haryana in India, as well as into Pakistan. This arid region is characterized by extreme temperatures, low and erratic rainfall, and sparse vegetation. The average annual rainfall in the Thar Desert ranges between 100 to 500 millimeters, with the western part receiving the least and the eastern part receiving relatively more (Singhvi and Kar, 2004). Despite these harsh conditions, the Thar Desert has been home to human settlements for millennia. The inhabitants have developed a range of traditional practices to conserve and manage natural resources, ensuring their survival and the sustainability of their environment.

Traditional ecological knowledge in the Thar Desert is deeply rooted in the region's history and culture (Mukhopadhyay, 2008). Historical records and oral traditions reveal a rich legacy of environmental stewardship practiced by various communities, including the Bishnois, Rajputs, and other indigenous groups (Cairns, 2020). These communities have relied on an intimate understanding of their environment, passed down through generations, to develop innovative solutions to the challenges posed by the desert landscape.

2. Water Conservation Practices:

Water is the most critical resource in the Thar Desert, and traditional methods of water conservation reflect this reality. Some of the most notable practices include:

- **Khadins:** These are ingenious runoff farming systems that harvest rainwater for agriculture. Constructed by building a bund (embankment) along the lower edges of sloping farmlands, khadins trap rainwater, allowing it to percolate and improve soil moisture. The system dates back to at least the 15th century and remains in use today.

- **Johads and Talabs:** These small and large ponds are dug to collect and store rainwater. Johads, in particular, are community-managed and play a vital role in groundwater recharge. There are approximately 5,000 johads in Alwar District alone, reflecting their widespread use and importance.

- **Baoris and Beris:** These are traditional step wells and shallow wells used for drinking water. They are often intricately designed and considered sacred in many communities. The famous step well, Chand Baori in Abhaneri, is an example of the sophisticated engineering of these structures.

3. Soil Conservation Techniques:

Soil erosion is a significant concern in the Thar Desert. Traditional practices to combat this include:

- **Bunds:** These small earthen embankments are constructed to prevent soil erosion and retain moisture in the soil. These bunds are often maintained collectively by village communities.

- **Agroforestry:** Integrating trees with crops and livestock farming helps in stabilizing the soil, reducing erosion, and providing shade and fodder. *Species like Prosopis cineraria (Khejri), Acacia nilotica (Babul), and Ziziphus mauritiana (Ber) are commonly used.*

- **Grass Strips:** Planting strips of grasses like vetiver helps in binding the soil and reducing wind and water erosion. These strips also serve as windbreaks, reducing the impact of sandstorms.

4. Biodiversity Conservation:

The people of the Thar Desert have developed various strategies to preserve their biodiversity:

4.1. Sacred Groves (Oran): Sacred groves, known locally as 'Oran', are patches of land preserved due to their religious significance. These groves serve as biodiversity hotspots, housing a variety of plant and animal species that are often not found in other parts of the desert (Agarwal, 2016). The protection of these groves is typically based on cultural and spiritual beliefs, which prohibit the cutting of trees, hunting of animals, or any form of exploitation of the natural resources within these areas.

- **Ramdevra Oran, Jaisalmer:** This sacred grove is dedicated to Baba Ramdev, a local deity revered by many communities in Rajasthan. The grove is a haven for native flora and fauna, including species like the Khejri tree (Prosopis cineraria), which is essential for maintaining the ecological balance in the desert. The grove also provides habitat for various bird species, reptiles, and small mammals, contributing to the region's biodiversity.

- **Mangala Devi Oran, Jaisalmer:** This sacred grove is associated with the worship of the goddess Mangala Devi. The grove is protected by the local community, who believe that harming the trees or wildlife within the grove would bring misfortune. The area supports a rich variety of plant species, including indigenous herbs and shrubs that have medicinal properties. The presence of undisturbed habitats within the grove also allows for the survival of several threatened and endemic species.

4.2. Community-managed Forests and Grazing Lands (Oran and Gauchar): Community-managed forests and grazing lands, known as 'Oran' and 'Gauchar' respectively, are integral to the traditional land management practices of the Thar Desert's inhabitants. These areas are collectively managed by local communities, ensuring sustainable use of resources while conserving biodiversity (Dhir et al., 2005).

- **Khejarli Oran, Jodhpur:** Famous for the Bishnoi community's sacrifice in 1730, where 363 Bishnois laid down their lives to protect Khejri trees. The grove is now a symbol of environmental conservation and a biodiversity hotspot. It supports a wide range of flora and fauna, including endangered species like the blackbuck (***Antilope cervicapra***) and chinkara (*Gazella bennettii*).

- **Rathnakar Oran, Barmer:** Managed by the Rathnakar community, this grove is rich in native tree species such as neem (*Azadirachta indica*) and ber (*Ziziphus mauritiana*). The community's traditional knowledge and collective efforts ensure the sustainable management of the forest, which also serves as a critical water catchment area.

4.3. Gauchar (Community Grazing Lands): These lands are specifically designated for grazing livestock, ensuring that there is enough fodder available throughout the year. The management practices include rotational grazing, which prevents overgrazing and promotes the growth of diverse plant species. This system supports the livelihoods of pastoral communities and helps maintain ecological balance. Gauchar lands in Alwar district is Known for their extensive johads (water harvesting structures), these lands support a variety of grasses and shrubs that are essential for livestock. The community management of these grazing lands ensures that they remain productive and resilient against the pressures of climate change and overgrazing.

4.4. Importance and Benefits:

- **Ecological Benefits:** Sacred groves and community-managed lands play a crucial role in conserving biodiversity. They act as refuges for various species of plants and animals, maintaining genetic diversity and ecological balance. These areas also contribute to soil conservation, water retention, and the overall health of the ecosystem.

- **Cultural and Spiritual Values:** The preservation of sacred groves and community-managed lands is deeply embedded in the cultural and spiritual beliefs of the local communities. This intrinsic value promotes respect for nature and encourages conservation practices that are sustainable and community-driven.

- **Livelihood Support:** The sustainable management of Oran and Gauchar lands supports the livelihoods of pastoral and agricultural communities. These areas provide essential resources such as fodder, fuel, and medicinal plants, which are crucial for the survival and well-being of the local population.

- **Climate Resilience:** By maintaining diverse and healthy ecosystems, sacred groves and community-managed lands enhance the resilience of the Thar Desert's environment against climate change. These areas serve as buffers against extreme weather events, such as droughts and sandstorms, thereby protecting the communities that depend on them.

5. Socio-Cultural and Spiritual Values:

The traditional practices of the Thar Desert are not merely practical solutions but are deeply intertwined with the socio-cultural and spiritual fabric of the communities (Parween, 2021). The reverence for nature is evident in the way religious beliefs and cultural practices promote conservation:

- **Bishnoi Community:** The Bishnois are known for their strict adherence to environmental conservation principles, guided by 29 religious tenets that include protecting trees and wildlife. Their practices have contributed significantly to the conservation of species like the blackbuck and chinkara.

- **Festivals and Rituals:** Many festivals and rituals in the Thar Desert are centered around the environment, celebrating the onset of monsoons, harvests, and other natural phenomena. Festivals like Teej and Gangaur involve rituals that emphasize the importance of natural elements like water and soil.

6. Contemporary Relevance and Challenges:

While traditional practices have proven their worth over centuries, they face several challenges in the contemporary context:

- **Modernization and Urbanization:** The shift towards modern agricultural practices and urbanization has led to the neglect of traditional methods. This shift threatens the sustainability of the region's ecosystems.

- **Climate Change:** Increasing temperatures and changing rainfall patterns pose new challenges that require adaptation and integration of traditional knowledge with modern scientific approaches. The Thar Desert is experiencing more frequent droughts and extreme weather events, necessitating innovative solutions.

- **Policy and Governance:** There is a need for policies that recognize and integrate traditional ecological knowledge into mainstream conservation and development strategies. Empowering local communities and involving them in decision-making processes is crucial for the success of these policies.

7. Conclusion:

The Thar Desert of Rajasthan presents a rich tapestry of ecological diversity, cultural heritage, and socio-economic resilience. The traditional practices of environmental conservation and management developed by the local communities are a testament to their ingenuity and deep connection with their environment. By embracing a holistic approach that integrates ecological, cultural, and socio-economic perspectives, policymakers and practitioners can work collaboratively with local communities to promote environmental sustainability, enhance livelihood resilience, and foster inclusive development in the Thar Desert and beyond. Continued research, dialogue, and action are essential to uphold the legacy of conservation and stewardship in this unique region, ensuring a harmonious coexistence between humanity and the natural world.

References:

1. Agarwal, M. (2016). Conserving water & biodiversity: traditions of sacred groves in India. *European Journal of Sustainable Development*, 5(4), 129-129.
2. Cairns, R. (2020). *Dharmic environmentalism: Hindu traditions and ecological care* (Doctoral dissertation, Memorial University of Newfoundland).
3. Dhir, R. P., Director, C. A. Z. R. I., & Colony, D. (2005). Some natural and anthropogenic specificities of the Thar. *Changing faunal ecology in Thar Desert. Scientific Publisher, Jodhpur, India*, 27-36.
4. Mukhopadhyay, D. (2008). Indigenous knowledge and sustainable natural resource management in the Indian desert. In *The Future of Drylands: International Scientific Conference on Desertification and Drylands Research Tunis, Tunisia, 19-21 June 2006* (pp. 161-170). Springer Netherlands.
5. Parween, R. (2021). *Traditional Knowledge and Practices, Sacred Spaces and Protected Areas: Their Success in Conserving Biodiversity* (Doctoral dissertation, University of York).
6. Singhvi, A. K., & Kar, A. (2004). The aeolian sedimentation record of the Thar Desert. *Journal of Earth System Science, 113*, 371-401.
7. Varghese, K. A. (2023). An Overview of World Deserts with Special Reference to Thar Desert. Natural Resource Management in the Thar Desert Region of Rajasthan, 1-24.

8. Role of Education in Promoting Sustainable Development

Sunanda Das

Ph.D. scholar, Tata Institute of Social Sciences Hyderabad

Email: hp2020ss008@stud.tiss.edu

Abstract:

The perception of sustainable development arose by way of a reply to a rising anxiety around humanoid civilization's influence on the usual setting. The idea of sustainable development remained clear in 1987 by the Brundtland Commission (officially the World Commission on Environment besides Development) by way of 'expansion that encounters the requirements of the contemporary deprived of co-operating the aptitude of imminent cohorts to encounter their individual essentials'. This meaning admits that although expansion could be essential to encounter humanoid requirements besides recover the excellence of lifespan, it necessity occur deprived of reducing the volume of the usual situation to encounter current besides upcoming requirements. The sustainable development drive has full-grown besides electioneered on the base that sustainability defends together the welfares of upcoming peers then the earth's volume to renew. At chief it highlighted the setting in growth rules but, meanwhile 2002, has changed to include communal fairness besides the contest in contradiction of lack by means of important philosophies of sustainable development. Decent excellence schooling is an indispensable instrument aimed at attaining an additional sustainable biosphere. This was accentuated at the UN World Summit in Johannesburg in 2002 wherever the reorientation of present schooling organizations remained delineated by way of noteworthy to sustainable development. Education for sustainable development (ESD) endorses the growth of the gen, services, sympathetic, standards besides movements obligatory to generate a sustainable world, which safeguards environmental defence besides upkeep, endorses communal even-handedness besides inspires financial sustainability. The idea of ESD industrialized mainly after ecological teaching, which consumes required to mature the information, services, standards, arrogances besides actions in persons to upkeep for their setting. The goal of ESD is to allow persons to brand choices besides transmit available movements to recover our excellence of lifetime deprived of co-operating the earth. It similarly purposes to participate the standards intrinsic in sustainable development hooked on completely characteristics besides stages of education. There are a amount of important tunes in ESD besides though the leading emphasis is on ecological anxieties, it too speeches melodies such by method of lack mitigation, nationality, concord, morals, accountability in native besides worldwide settings, equality besides supremacy, impartiality, humanoid privileges, sex parity, business accountability, usual reserve organization besides organic variety. It is typically recognized that convinced physiognomies are imperative aimed at the positive employment of ESD, sparkly the equivalent position of together the knowledge procedure besides the consequences of the teaching procedure.

Keywords: Embedded in the curriculum, Endorse perilous rational, Employ a diversity of instructive methods, Permit apprentices to contribute in decision-making, Appearance to the future'

1. Introduction:

The association amid ecological teaching, teaching for sustainable development besides growth teaching is multifaceted, besides the three repeatedly show additional resemblances than changes (Becker, 2023). Altogether three are fundamentally worried by social alteration finished teaching then the raise of standards, insolences besides empathetic. An essential worth endorsed through the three subdivisions is admiration: admiration for physically, admiration for others, admiration aimed at the biosphere we are living in besides do admiration aimed at the earth. Though, an earlier inspection of both subdivisions proposes that both consume a main goal or emphasis that circles it separately after the others. Ecological teaching industrialized after the anxiety that humanoid growth was consuming deeply harmful belongings on the normal setting also its main goal is the defence besides upkeep of the setting counting usual homes besides bionetworks (Marran, 2017). Growth teaching's main anxiety is the discount of deficiency, the elevation of communal fairness besides the development of excellence of lifetime aimed at persons. It speeches rudimentary humanoid requirements besides relations native besides worldwide movements. Growth teaching emphases on interdependence besides interconnectedness amid persons on together a worldwide in addition to native viewpoint nonetheless fixes not usually spread this to bionetwork interdependence or exact ecological anxieties. DE chiefly emphases on community subjects of humanoid privileges, communal unfairness, humanoid deficiency besides ecosphere nationality. It is troubled through the structure of information, sympathetic, services, arrogances, standards besides actions compulsory to empower individuals to judgementally inspect the biosphere, its expansion besides to entertainment to brand it a supplementary impartial besides reasonable residence. It consumes abundant in shared by additional procedures of communal besides party-political teaching (DCI, 2003). Humanoid privileges teaching, concord instruction, diverse tutoring, teaching on contest besides competition matters, ecological teaching in addition to eventually nationality schooling all must meeting topographies besides anxieties through growth teaching, though both consumes its individual separate charm besides emphasis. Teaching for sustainable development's principal anxiety is the development of the excellence of age aimed at persons deprived of harmful the site (Farr, 2010). So however altogether three 'educations' necessity plentiful in communal they vary in their chief box. The connotation among ESD also extra informative subdivisions is the subject of continuing conversation finished the previous recurrently about ESD by method of being 'stocks of' their education. Also, what many respect by way of the neighbouring subdivision to ESD - ecological teaching - is not unavoidably gratified to be understood as a corresponding to ESD. Numerous trusts that ESD must hold all these instructive subdivisions to a convinced equal besides, through supportable growth presumptuous cumulative rank in rule besides instructive settings, there will be an essential aimed at all of these subdivisions besides their GPs to travel additional carefully the unities amid them.

Edification for sustainable development increases upon the shared besides hominid privileges measurement in DE besides additional informative subdivisions to comprise a sturdy ecological emphasis. ESD stocks numerous comparisons through DE then speeches subjects for example temperature modification, emollient scarcities, marine contamination, the necessity to continue biodiversity in addition to deficiency lessening besides hominoid privileges. ESD besides DE correspondingly engagement comparable practises counting: dangerous rational besides problematic resolving, experimental education, character production, directed clarification, argument, commodities rational besides participating conclusion creation. ESD likewise assistances to grow relations amid the exists of persons nearby besides in the emerging biosphere besides inspires us to connection our movements at a native equal to the wants then organization of the earth besides its populace. The fundamental values of ESD by way of drew by UNESCO highpoint the rank of admiration besides upkeep aimed at lifetime in altogether its varied procedures: this includes the defence then refurbishment of the soil's bionetworks, admiration aimed at the self-esteem then humanoid privileges of persons, admiration aimed at the privileges of upcoming peers then admiration aimed at national variety. Happening the foundation of the inter-sectorial relations labelled overhead container, ESD is the umbrella intended at countless of the additional 'schoolings' or is ESD an component of all these 'teachings'.

2. Edification/Education by Way of Substance Aimed at Sustainable Development:

The Prospectus Outline for Education aimed at Sustainable Development (ESD) assistances to device the nationwide strategy (Oyedepo et al., 2018). It is an influence to the novel UNESCO Global Action Programme on Education for Sustainable Development next the UNESD-decade besides to the United Nation's 2030-agenda through the sustainable development goals (SDGs). Its emphasis is on safeguarding that – in eras of increasing worldwide tests – excellence of university teaching develops the basis for sustainable development. Prospectus Outline must be spoke then applied thru the optional student-oriented methods. A chiefly significant influence to instructive alteration is a shared contract on standards besides objects. Such a contract container be understood in the worldwide group's resolve on Sustainable development Goals (SDGs) then in the UNESCO instincts aimed at the application of the Programme 2030 in tutoring. This straightforward empathetic is essential to the Prospectus Agenda besides canister likewise stand create in the worldwide and German labours to device the UNESCO Global Action Programme on Schooling for Sustainable Development. In a progressively globalised ecosphere, the philosophies of sustainable development need developed the dominant standards of a susceptible besides tremendously scarce atmosphere besides mortality Ramlogan, (2004). The Program 2030 has acknowledged sustainable development to remain the combined detached of the 17SDGs. The Programme associations this important belief to the worldwide humanoid privileges besides to the knowledge impartial of universal population. The sense of education meant on the accomplishment of the SDGs is tinted then strong-minded through board 4.7. Now, Education for Sustainable Development (ESD) is stated by way of an important tool aimed at attaining these goalmouths. It is a anxiety of the Prospectus/Curriculum Outline to attach dissimilar instructive civilizations similar Ecological Education besides Worldwide Knowledge inside ESD. In the wanted alteration procedure the complete maintainable growth code determination is the worth middle then shared preliminary opinion of altogether school/college topics besides university doings (see Fig-1).

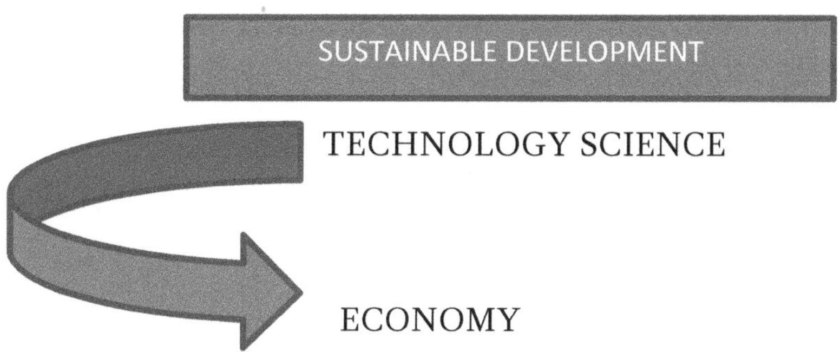

Fig: 1-Education by way of substance aimed at Sustainable Development

3. Worldwide Growth Teaching in the Setting of Teaching for Sustainable Development:

Different in the old-style school topics, Global Development Education requirements to be labelled, i.e. the test of global development in interpretation of our sustainability (Pepper, 1999). Global alteration - a test aimed at our volume to slender). While university topics are obviously absorbed on unique or additional orientation disciplines, Global Development Education is mostly clear thru:

- Resolves on global besides nationwide heights in dissimilar turfs of government, chiefly expansion, and financial, communal then conservational government.
- Technical philosophy then present examines of pertinent disciplines in these arenas as well as of instructive educations.
- Stresses of location and requirement concerning globalisation then sustainable development, on the heights of civilization then the separate.
- The orientation to purposes of sustainable development in addition to ideas besides packages of Education for Sustainable Development.
- The compatibility through the moralistic thoughts of complex conservatory themes.

4. The Connection of Varied Constructions in the Sequence of Lively Globalisation:

Procedures of globalisation remain existence armour-plated through practical novelty besides through financial besides party-political welfares. On the newest meanwhile the European settlement of the biosphere, procedures of globalisation can be saw. They must been raced up significantly throughout the historical periods then frequently self-governing supremacy then legislature cannot save step by these procedures. We container sign opposite tendencies in globalisation: On the one pointer, consistent belongings are rising through worldwide procedures. Mostly the doings of international commercial companies besides businesses in the lawns of cash, ability, communication, and then publicity before movable continue responsible envisioned meant at these possessions. Buildings or universal webs rise through unvarying effort styles, expert values, alike structural constructions then standards. Communal nets usual values aimed at message, outline aesthetics etc. then proposal ground-breaking international commercial replicas. By way of by part cheap, wanted aimed at sustainability goalmouths similar distribution then reserve upkeep strength reduction through the curb.

5. Equilibrium Amid International Besides Native:

The significance of local, regional and national levels is underscored in the international sustainability resolutions (Huck and Kurkin, 2018). Personal chances for participation as well as accessible institutions and persons at all levels constitute an important potential for confidence, in view of largely anonymous global structures and relationships. In addition to opening up this potential, the interactions require new procedures for coordination among the areas for which various actors, such as corporations, political institutions, non-governmental organisations etc., are responsible. In this context the World Bank refers to "social capital", which consists of social networks and their institutional and cultural bases, being decisive for coherent development processes in the sustainability dimensions. Composed by the global public of conditions, Germany is dedicated to:

- The contest in contradiction of deficiency
- Concord, liberty, equality besides humanoid privileges (education, food safety)
- A reasonable enterprise of globalisation besides
- The safeguarding of atmosphere besides normal possessions.

6. Sustainable Development Goals (SDGs):

- Surface absence in overall its events universally
- Surface hunger, attain nourishment safety besides better-quality nourishment besides endorse maintainable farming
- Safeguard fit exists then endorse happiness aimed at all at all eternities
- Guarantee wide-ranging then reasonable excellence education besides endorse enduring/ education   information chances aimed at altogether.

7. Conclusion:

The rank of an alteration of belvedere in ESD/Global Development Education dishonesties in the inaugural of gaps (hiatus) of insight aimed at the dissimilar. The annoyance linked through this alteration unlocks the accidental aimed at an aware insight of one's personal rational then of realisms after an unacquainted opinion of opinion. An alteration of belvederes needs then ropes the skill to stand uncertainties, the aptitude to suitably decrease difficulties, besides the aptitude to disapprovingly assess conditions.

Reference(s):

1. Becker, P. (2023). *Sustainability science: Managing risk and resilience for sustainable development.* Elsevier.
2. Brundtland, G (ed.) (1987). Our Common Future: The World Commission on Environment and Development, Oxford: Oxford University Press.

3. Comhar, SDC (2007). Recommendations on the Review of the National Sustainable Development Strategy, Dublin.

4. DCI, Department of Foreign Affairs (2003) describing...understanding...challenging...the story of human development in today's world, Development Cooperation Ireland.

5. Department of Education and Science (DES) (2004). A Brief Description of the Irish Education System, Government of Ireland.

6. Department of the Environment and Heritage (2006). Caring for Our Future: The Australian Government Strategy for the UNDESD 2005-2014.

7. ECO-UNESCO (2007). available: http://www.ecounesco.ie.ECO-UNESCO (2007) Research Project on Education for Sustainable Development in Ireland, commissioned by Comhar SDC, Dublin.

8. Farr, S. (2010). *Teaching as leadership: The highly effective teacher's guide to closing the achievement gap.* John Wiley & Sons.

9. Finnish National Commission on Sustainable Development (2006) Strategy for Education and Training for Sustainable Development and Implementation Plan 2006-2014, Finland.

10. Huck, W., & Kurkin, C. (2018). The UN Sustainable Development Goals (SDGs) in the transnational multilevel system. Heidelberg Journal of International Law (HJIL)/Zeitschrift für ausländisches öffentliches Recht und Völkerrecht (ZaöRV), 2, 375.

11. Marran, C. L. (2017). *Ecology without culture: Aesthetics for a toxic world.* U of Minnesota Press.

12. Ministerie van LNV (2004). Learning for Sustainable Development: From the Margins to the Mainstream, The Netherlands.

13. Oyedepo, S. O., Babalola, O. P., Nwanya, S. C., Kilanko, O., Leramo, R. O., Aworinde, A. K., ... & Agberegha, O. L. (2018). Towards a sustainable electricity supply in nigeria: the role of decentralized renewable energy system. *European Journal of Sustainable development research, 2*(4), 40.

14. Pepper, D. (1999). Ecological modernisation or the 'ideal model'of sustainable development? Questions prompted at Europe's periphery. *Environmental politics, 8*(4), 1-34.

15. Ramlogan, R. (2004). *The developing world and the environment: Making the case for effective protection of the global environment.* University Press of America.

16. The Sustainable Development Education Panel (2003) Learning to Last: The Government's Sustainable Development Education Draft Strategy for England, London.Ubuntu Network (2007), available: http://www.ubuntu.ie.

17. UNECE (2005). Strategy for Education for Sustainable Development, available: http://www.unece.org/env/documents/2005/cep/ac.13/cep.ac.13.2005.3.rev.1... (accessed November 2007).

18. UNECE (n.d.) (2007). "Good Practices' in Education for Sustainable Development in theUNECERegion',questionnaire,available:http://www.unece.org/env/esd/inf.meeting.docs/Bureau/Good%20practices.templ.pdf (accessed February 2007).

19. UNESCO (2006). International Implementation Scheme for the Decade in Brief, available:http://portal.unesco.org/education/en/ev.phpURL_ID=23280&URL_DO=DO_TOPI.

9. Economic Impacts of Biodiversity Loss and Conservation Strategies

Vishal Singh[1], Dr. Rajeev Kumar Chaudhary[2]

[1]Assistant Professor, Vivek College of Law, Bijnor

Email: vishalsinghdxn@gmail.com

[2]Principal, Vivek College of Law, Bijnor

Email: Rjv.bjn@gmail.com

Abstract:

Biodiversity loss isn't just an environmental concern, it's a significant economic threat. Our economies rely heavily on the vast array of services provided by ecosystems - from fertile soil and clean water to pollination and natural pest control. But human activities like habitat destruction and overexploitation are pushing species towards extinction at an alarming rate. This decline in biodiversity comes with a hefty price tag. Reduced biodiversity disrupts essential ecological processes, impacting agriculture, fisheries, and forestry. We lose the natural checks and balances that keep pests in line, requiring us to spend more on pesticides. Furthermore, the pool of genetic diversity shrinks, limiting our options for developing new crops and medicines. The good news is that conservation efforts can mitigate these economic losses. Strategies like creating protected areas and implementing sustainable resource management practices not only safeguard species but also generate economic benefits. Ecotourism, for instance, thrives on healthy ecosystems with diverse wildlife. Additionally, putting a proper value on ecosystem services through mechanisms like payments for environmental services can incentivize communities to conserve their natural resources. The challenge lies in addressing the root causes of biodiversity loss. Unsustainable practices driven by factors like short-sighted policies and perverse incentives need to be reformed. Integrating biodiversity considerations into economic decision-making is crucial for a future where a thriving economy coexists with a healthy planet.

Keywords: Biodiversity loss, Ecosystem Services, Habitat, Sustainable Resource, Exponential Population, conservation strategies.

1.Introduction:

Imagine a vibrant shade woven from in numerous vestments, each representing a unique species on Earth. This shade, biodiversity, isn't just a beautiful display of life's variety; it's the veritably foundation of a healthy earth and the well- being of all living effects, including us. But this intricate shade is facing a growing trouble biodiversity loss (Loeks, 2020). Biodiversity loss refers to the decline in the variety of life at all situations – genes, species, and ecosystems. It encompasses the extermination of species, the drop in population sizes of being species, and the declination of territories that support them (Heydari et al., 2020). This decline is passing at an unknown rate, far exceeding what is considered natural. While extermination is a natural process, the current rate is estimated to be hundreds to thousands of times faster than the background rate.

The causes of this rapid-fire decline are multitudinous, but utmost stem from mortal conditioning. Habitat loss and declination are leading lawbreakers. timbers are cleared for husbandry, development, and resource birth, leaving creatures and shops with nowhere to go. also, overexploitation of coffers like fish and timber pushes species to the point of collapse. Invasive species, introduced accidentally or designedly, disrupt ecological balance by outcompeting native species for coffers. Pollution, another major motorist, contaminates air, water, and soil, harming delicate ecosystems and hindering the growth and survival of shops and creatures (Aftab and Hakeem, 2023). Climate change, caused by hothouse gas emigrations, further exacerbates biodiversity loss by altering rainfall patterns, melting glaciers, and raising ocean situations. These changes disrupt territories and make it delicate for species to acclimatize)Shivanna, 2022).

The consequences of biodiversity loss are far- reaching and profound. From a practical viewpoint, it disrupts the intricate web of life that sustains us. Ecosystems with high biodiversity give essential services like clean air and water, pollination of crops, and natural pest control (Ali and Kamraju, 2023). With smaller species, these services come less effective, risking food security, water quality, and mortal health. The loss of biodiversity also represents a loss of irreplaceable inheritable information. Every species is a unique force of genes, some with implicit operations in drug, husbandry, and bioengineering. As species vanish, we lose the eventuality to develop new medicines, produce more flexible crops, and understand the intricate mechanisms of life on Earth. Beyond the practical aspects, biodiversity loss signifies a loss of wonder and beauty. Each species has a unique story, a part to play in the grand shade of life. The exposure of a species diminishes the uproariousness of our earth and the eventuality for unborn generations to witness nature's inconceivable diversity. Understanding the causes and consequences of biodiversity loss is pivotal for chancing results. The ensuing sections will claw deeper into the factors driving this decline and explore strategies for conservation – a critical trouble to mend the unraveling shade of life on Earth.

2. Acknowledgment:

At the end of journey if this research project from the beginning until the date of completion, I have come across several people, a variety of experiences and a lot of effort. Today, I would like to mention all those who have been, directly or indirectly, of great support to me and my work.I would like to express my gratitude, especially to my friends and colleagues who, having been experienced in the field, helped me understand the concept and its relevance. I would like to thank my family. Without their adoration and assistance, I am nothing. My parent's blessings are something I owe them. The cooperation and direction of my parents enabled me to get an education of this level, and their blessings inspired me to complete this work.

3. Objective:

Objectives are following:

- To study biodiversity loss
- To study conservation strategies

4. Hypothesis:

This research has been conducted with a view to testing the hypothesis formulated as follows: The conservation strategies in all over the world play a significant role in the protection of the biodiversity.

5. Statement of the problem:

There is a biodiversity catastrophe on Earth right now. Because of things like pollution, climate change, unsustainable resource use, invasive species, and habitat loss from deforestation and urbanization, species are disappearing at a startling rate. Entire ecosystems are at risk due to this deterioration, which also interferes with natural processes that provide us access to food security, clean water and air, and necessary medications. It also creates a vicious loop by making ecosystems less resilient to climate change. In order to alleviate this situation, conservation techniques are essential. It is crucial to preserve and restore natural ecosystems, which calls for creative solutions like setting up protected areas and animal corridors. Minimizing our environmental impact requires the use of sustainable resource management techniques. Since climate change is a primary cause of biodiversity loss, combating it is essential. Long-term success also depends on increasing public awareness and encouraging individual action, such as cutting back on consumption and supporting sustainable enterprises. We cannot stop the loss of biodiversity and guarantee a healthy world for future generations unless we adopt a comprehensive and cooperative strategy.

6. Declaration of Interest Statement:

There is no conflict of interest as per the financial statement, and the manuscript has been published only for academic purposes.

7. Historical Background of Biodiversity Loss:

The story of biodiversity loss isn't a recent one. Earth has witnessed five major extinction events throughout its history, each wiping out a significant portion of existing life (Elewa and Abdelhady, 2020). These events were primarily caused by natural disasters like asteroid impacts or massive volcanic eruptions. However, the focus today is on the anthropogenic extinction, the current rapid decline driven by human activities. While the impact of humans on biodiversity can be traced back thousands of years, the most significant changes started happening in the last few centuries. Here's a historical glimpse:

Early Impacts (Pre-Industrial Revolution):

- Hunting and Overexploitation: Early human populations played a role in the extinction of large mammals like mammoths and saber-toothed tigers. As humans migrated across continents, their hunting practices put pressure on local fauna.
- Habitat Alteration: The shift from nomadic lifestyles to agriculture led to deforestation and land use changes, impacting local ecosystems.

Industrial Revolution and Beyond (18th Century Onwards):

- Exponential Population Growth: The Industrial Revolution fueled a significant rise in human population. This growing population demanded more resources, leading to increased pressure on land and wildlife.
- Habitat Destruction: Deforestation for agriculture, timber, and development accelerated at an alarming rate.
- Resource Depletion: Unsustainable fishing practices and industrial resource extraction put immense pressure on specific species and ecosystems.
- Invasive Species: Global trade and travel facilitated the unintentional introduction of non-native species that disrupted established ecological balances.
- Pollution: Industrialization led to increased air, water, and soil pollution, harming wildlife and disrupting ecosystems.

20th and 21st Centuries: Recognizing the Crisis:

- Scientific Evidence: The 20th century saw a growing understanding

- of the interconnectedness of ecosystems and the vital role of biodiversity. Scientific studies began highlighting the alarming rate of species decline.
- Conservation Movements: Public awareness about biodiversity loss
- led to the rise of conservation movements and international environmental agreements.
- New Threats: Climate change emerged as a major driver of biodiversity loss, altering habitats and disrupting ecological processes at a global scale.

The historical background of biodiversity loss shows a progressively intensifying impact of human activities. While early humans interacted with their environment, the industrial revolution and its aftermath marked a turning point (Ellis, 2021). Today, we stand at a critical juncture, needing to learn from the past mistakes and implement effective conservation strategies to prevent a major extinction event driven by human actions.

8. Current Scenario of Biodiversity Loss in India:

India, a landmass boasting exceptional biodiversity, is unfortunately facing a significant decline in its rich variety of life (Halder and Jha, 2023). Here's a look at the current scenario of biodiversity loss in India:

I.   Habitat Loss and Degradation: India's biodiversity hotspots, crucial cradles of species diversity, have been severely impacted. A staggering 90% of the area under these hotspots has been lost due to deforestation, infrastructure development, and unsustainable resource extraction.

II. Species in Peril: The International Union for Conservation of Nature (IUCN) Red List paints a worrying picture. Over 12% of the 1,212 animal species monitored in India are classified as endangered, including iconic animals like the Bengal Tiger and the Indian Elephant. At least 25 species have already gone extinct within these hotspots.

III. Pollution's Impact: Uncontrolled industrial activity and agricultural practices contribute significantly to air, water, and soil pollution. This contamination disrupts ecosystems and harms wildlife populations.

IV. Climate Change: India's diverse ecosystems, from the Himalayas to the coastal regions, are increasingly vulnerable due to climate change. Rising temperatures, erratic weather patterns, and melting glaciers pose a major threat to species and their habitats.

V.   Uneven Distribution of Impacts: The burden of biodiversity loss isn't equally shared. Fragile ecosystems in the Northeast and Western Ghats are particularly at risk.

Additionally, communities heavily reliant on natural resources for their livelihoods are most affected by the decline in biodiversity.

VI. Despite this grim scenario, there are rays of hope.

VII. Conservation Efforts: India has a network of protected areas like national parks and wildlife sanctuaries that play a crucial role in safeguarding biodiversity. Efforts are underway to promote sustainable resource management practices and address human-wildlife conflict.

VIII. Community Involvement: Local communities are increasingly being involved in conservation initiatives, recognizing their vital role in protecting natural resources.

IX. Public Awareness: Growing public awareness about the importance of biodiversity is driving support for conservation efforts.

X. The current situation in India demands immediate and decisive action. By prioritizing habitat restoration, promoting sustainable development, and fostering community participation, India can strive to reverse the tide of biodiversity loss and conserve its irreplaceable natural heritage.

9. Economic Impacts of Biodiversity:

The profitable impacts of biodiversity loss are vast and far- reaching. Our husbandry are intricately linked to the health and functioning of ecosystems, and biodiversity decline disrupts these essential processes, leading to a range of profitable consequences also is a breakdown of some pivotal areas:

I. Loss of Ecosystem Services: Food Security Pollinators like sundries and butterflies are vital for multitudinous crops. Declines in these species can lead to lower yields and advanced food prices. also, healthy ecosystems give natural pest control services, reducing dependence on pesticides and their associated costs. Water Security timbers play a vital part in regulating water cycles. With deforestation, water filtration and sanctification capabilities decline, leading to increased water failure and treatment costs. Coastal Protection Mangroves and coral reefs act as natural walls against cataracts and storms. Their declination increases the vulnerability of coastal communities to cyclones and lathers, leading to significant profitable losses.

II. Resource Depletion: Overfishing Unsustainable fishing practices deplete fish stocks, reducing catches and impacting livelihoods in fishing communities. also, it disrupts marine ecosystems, affecting other species that calculate on fish. Deforestation Unsustainable logging practices reduce timber vacuity and quality, leading to advanced prices and potentially affecting industriousness like furniture manufacturing.

III. Increased Costs of results: Pollution Cleanup Pollution from artificial exertion and husbandry disrupts ecosystems and requires precious remittal sweats. Disaster Management Habitat declination increases the trouble and strictness of natural disasters, leading to advanced costs for disaster operation and recovery.

IV. Reduced Tourism Revenue: Ecotourism Thriving ecosystems with different wildlife attract sightseers, generating profit for original communities. Biodiversity loss diminishes the appeal of these destinations, impacting tourism income.

V. Loss of Implicit Benefits: New Medicines multitudinous medicines are derived from natural sources. With species decimation, we lose the eventuality to discover new drugs and treatments.

Biomimicry Studying nature's inventions inspires technological advancements. Biodiversity loss reduces this implicit source of relief. The profitable costs of biodiversity loss are significant, estimated to be in the trillions of bones annually. It's not just about environmental protection; it's about securing the truly foundation of a healthy and prosperous economy.

10. Comparative Study of USA and UK with India:

All three nations – the USA, UK, and India – face significant challenges with biodiversity loss, but the specific drivers and impacts vary due to differences in geography, development stage, and historical context. Here's a breakdown for each country:

- *USA:*

  Drivers: Habitat loss due to agriculture and urban sprawl, invasive species, pollution, and climate change.

  Impacts: Decline in pollinators like bees and butterflies, freshwater species like amphibians and mussels, and grassland birds. Reduced resilience to natural disasters like floods and droughts.

  Conservation Efforts: Network of national parks and wildlife refuges, Endangered Species Act, and growing focus on sustainable agriculture.

- *UK:*

  Drivers: Historically, extensive habitat loss for agriculture and industrialization. Currently, fragmentation of remaining habitats, intensification of agriculture, and climate change are key threats.

Impacts: Loss of native species like hedgehogs and butterflies. Marine ecosystems are also under pressure from overfishing and pollution.

Conservation Efforts: Efforts to restore native habitats, reintroduce species, and promote sustainable farming practices.

- *India:*

Drivers: Habitat loss due to deforestation, infrastructure development, and unsustainable resource extraction. Pollution from industrial activities and agriculture. Climate change poses a growing threat to diverse ecosystems.

Impacts: High rate of species decline in biodiversity hotspots like the Western Ghats and Northeast India. Endangered iconic species like Bengal Tiger and Indian Elephant.

Conservation Efforts: Network of protected areas, initiatives for sustainable resource management, and growing public awareness about the importance of biodiversity.

Comparison Points:

Extent of Loss: India, with its rich biodiversity hotspots, might be experiencing a faster rate of species decline compared to the USA and UK, which have already lost significant habitat in the past.

Drivers: The USA's primary threats lie in habitat conversion and invasive species, while the UK faces challenges with agricultural intensification and habitat fragmentation. India confronts a complex mix of factors, including habitat loss, pollution, and climate change.

Conservation Efforts: All three countries have protected areas and endangered species legislation. However, India is increasingly focusing on community involvement and sustainable resource management practices.

Looking Forward:

Combating biodiversity loss requires a global effort. All three nations can learn from each other's conservation strategies and work collaboratively to address shared threats like climate change. Implementing policies that promote sustainable development, fostering public awareness, and supporting research on biodiversity conservation are crucial steps for all three countries.

11. Conservation strategies:

The decline of biodiversity is a complex issue, but there are a multitude of strategies we can employ to mitigate it and promote the recovery of our planet's rich tapestry of life. Here's a look at some key approaches:

I. *Protecting Habitats:*

Establishing Protected Areas: Creating national parks, wildlife sanctuaries, and other protected areas is essential for safeguarding critical habitats and the species that depend on them.

Habitat Restoration: Restoring degraded habitats by planting native trees, removing invasive species, and reconnecting fragmented landscapes allows species populations to recover and thrive.

Corridor Creation: Establishing wildlife corridors that connect fragmented habitats allows animals to move freely between areas, promoting genetic diversity and population health.

II. *Sustainable Resource Management:*

Sustainable Forestry: Implementing practices like selective logging and reforestation ensures the long-term health of forests and minimizes their loss.

Sustainable Fishing: Setting quotas, implementing gear restrictions, and protecting breeding grounds are crucial for maintaining healthy fish populations and preventing overfishing.

Sustainable Agriculture: Techniques like crop rotation, cover cropping, and integrated pest management can reduce reliance on harmful pesticides and fertilizers, minimizing their impact on biodiversity.

III. *Addressing Threats:*

Controlling Invasive Species: Preventing the introduction and spread of invasive species through regulations and control measures is vital for protecting native ecosystems.

Combating Pollution: Implementing stricter regulations on air, water, and soil pollution, along with promoting cleaner technologies and waste management practices, is essential.

Mitigating Climate Change: Reducing greenhouse gas emissions to combat climate change is crucial for protecting ecosystems and the species that depend on specific climatic conditions.

IV. *Species-Specific Conservation:*

Captive Breeding and Reintroduction Programs: These programs can be crucial for critically endangered species, helping to rebuild populations and reintroduce them to their natural habitats when feasible.

Endangered Species Legislation: Laws that protect endangered species and their habitats are important tools for preventing extinction.

V.   *Public Awareness and Education:*

Educating the Public: Fostering public understanding of the importance of biodiversity and the threats it faces is crucial for gaining support for conservation efforts.

Promoting Sustainable Practices: Encouraging individuals to adopt sustainable practices in their daily lives, such as reducing consumption and minimizing waste, can collectively have a significant impact.

VI.   *Economic Incentives:*

Payments for Ecosystem Services: Programs that provide financial rewards to communities for protecting natural resources and maintaining ecosystem services can create economic incentives for conservation.

Sustainable Markets: Encouraging markets that value sustainable products and practices can incentivize businesses to adopt environmentally friendly approaches.

Moving Forward Conservation strategies need to be comprehensive, addressing the root causes of biodiversity loss while also focusing on species protection and habitat restoration (Hermoso et al., 2022). Collaboration between governments, NGOs, local communities, and businesses is critical for successful implementation. By working together, we can find innovative solutions and ensure a future where a thriving human society coexists with a healthy and diverse natural world.

12. Conclusion:

Biodiversity loss isn't just an environmental concern; it's a threat to human well-being and economic prosperity. The decline of species and ecosystems disrupts the very foundation of life on Earth, impacting everything from food security and clean water to climate regulation and natural disaster resilience. The economic costs are staggering, with lost ecosystem services and the potential for future discoveries adding to the burden. However, there's still hope. By implementing a range of conservation strategies, we can start to mend the unraveling tapestry of life. Protecting habitats through a network of protected areas and habitat restoration efforts is crucial. Sustainable resource management practices in forestry, agriculture, and fishing are essential for minimizing human impact. Addressing threats like invasive species, pollution, and climate change is a collective responsibility. Species-specific conservation programs offer a lifeline for critically endangered creatures. Ultimately, the future of biodiversity lies at a crossroads. We can choose to continue on the current path, with potentially devastating consequences. Or, we can embrace a new path of sustainable practices, conservation efforts, and collaboration. By taking action now, we can safeguard the incredible diversity of life on Earth, ensuring a healthy planet for ourselves and future generations. The choice is ours

References:

1. Aftab, T., & Hakeem, K. R. (Eds.). (2023). *Environmental Pollution Impact on Plants: Survival Strategies Under Challenging Conditions.* CRC Press.
2. Ali, M. A., & Kamraju, M. (2023). Ecosystem services. In *Natural Resources and Society: Understanding the Complex Relationship Between Humans and the Environment* (pp. 51-63). Cham: Springer Nature Switzerland.
3. Dasgupta, P. (2024). *The economics of biodiversity.* cambridge university Press.
4. Elewa, A. M., & Abdelhady, A. A. (2020). Past, present, and future mass extinctions. *Journal of African Earth Sciences, 162,* 103678.
5. Ellis, E. C. (2021). Land use and ecological change: A 12,000-year history. *Annual Review of Environment and Resources, 46*(1), 1-33.
6. Halder, M., & Jha, S. (2023). The current status of population extinction and biodiversity crisis of medicinal plants. In *Medicinal Plants: Biodiversity, Biotechnology and Conservation* (pp. 3-38). Singapore: Springer Nature Singapore.
7. Hermoso, V., Carvalho, S. B., Giakoumi, S., Goldsborough, D., Katsanevakis, S., Leontiou, S., ... & Yates, K. L. (2022). The EU Biodiversity Strategy for 2030: Opportunities and challenges on the path towards biodiversity recovery. *Environmental Science & Policy, 127,* 263-271.
8. Heydari, M., Omidipour, R., & Greenlee, J. (2020). Biodiversity, a review of the concept, measurement, opportunities, and challenges. *Journal of Wildlife and Biodiversity, 4*(4), 26-39.
9. Loeks, Z. (2020). *The Edible Ecosystem Solution: Growing Biodiversity in Your Backyard and Beyond.* New Society Publishers.5.
10. Shivanna, K. R. (2022). Climate change and its impact on biodiversity and human welfare. *Proceedings of the Indian National Science Academy, 88*(2), 160-171.

10. Eightfold Way for Meson and Baryon and Its Octonion Representation

Arun Kumar Rathore* and B. C. Chanyal**

Department of Physics, G. B. Pant University of Agriculture and Technology,

Pant Nagar 263145, Uttarakhand, India

Email: * arunkumarrathore706@gmail.com

**bcchanyal@gmail.com

Abstract:

In the present study, a connection between octonions and the SU(3) group wis established in order to produce a thorough analysis of the quark-flavor theory in the context of complex octonionic space. In order to indicate the three discrete isospin spaces, we build three sets of operators in complex octonion space. The fundamental (triplet) representation of the $SU(3)_f$ group is shown in order to describe the octonion three-isospin frames. Furthermore, we have described baryonic and mesonic octet representations within these isospin frames to illustrate the importance of the complexified octonion space.

Keywords: SU(3) group, The quark model, **Eightfold Way**

1. Introduction:

As far as we know, there are only four fundamental forces in nature i.e., gravitational, electromagnetic, weak, and strong in the order of increasing strength (Peskin and Schroeder, 1996). There is a physical theory that applies to each of these forces. Of course, Newton's law of universal gravitation is the foundation of the classical theory of gravity. Einstein's general theory of relativity (geometrodynamics would be a better term), is its relativistic generalisation (Griffiths, 1987). Since no complete quantum theory of gravity has yet been developed, most experts now believe that gravity is too weak to have any major impact on elementary particle physics. The physical theory that describes electromagnetic forces is called electrodynamics. Maxwell over one hundred years ago gave it its traditional formulation, special relativity, which was in reality the primary motivation for Maxwell's theory, was already consistent with it (Weinberg, 1995). Tomonaga, Feynman, and Schwinger (Anishetty et al., 2009) worked together in the 1940s to perfect the quantum theory of electrodynamics. Since the weak forces were unknown to classical physics, their theoretical explanation was given a relativistic quantum formulation from the beginning. The weak forces, which are responsible for nuclear beta decay (as well as, as we have seen, the decay of the pion, the muon (Marshak and Bethe, 1988), and many other unusual particles), are also responsible for the decay of many weird particles. Fenni initially proposed the idea of weak forces in 1933; it was further developed by Lee and Yang, Feynman and Gell-Mann, and many others in the 1950s; and it was finally given its current shape by Glashow, Weinberg, and Salam in the 1960s. The theory of weak interactions is sometimes referred to as flavordynamics for reasons that will become clear in due course. In the GWS model, electromagnetic and weak interactions are viewed as various expressions of a single electroweak force, hence the four forces are reduced to three. Regarding the strong forces (Conversi, Pancini and Piccioni, 1947), there actually wasn't any theory beyond Yukawa's revolutionary work from 1934 until the discovery of chromodynamics in the 1970s. Each of these forces is mediated by the exchange of a particle.

The graviton mediates gravitational forces, while the photon mediates electromagnetic forces, the gluon mediates strong forces, and the intermediate vector bosons W and Z mediate weak forces. These intermediaries act as carriers for the transfer of force between quarks or leptons. In theory, the force of impact between a bat and a baseball is nothing more than the result of the interaction between the quarks and leptons in each object. More specifically, the strong force, which Yukawa believed to be a fundamental and irreducible process, between two protons, for example, must be viewed as a complex interaction of six quarks. Clearly, this is not where you should search for simplicity. Instead, we must examine the force between two truly elementary particles in order to start. Hadrons can be categorised into hexagonal and triangular structures using the Eightfold Way. A question arose, why are the particles in a multiplet, which would ordinarily appear to be separate, regarded as several states of a single entity? This indicates that there are additional fundamental particles that each particle in the SU(3) multiplet is composed of. These basic particles were referred to as quarks by Gell-Mann (Gell-Mann and Zweig, 1964). The quark model of hadrons is the model of hadrons that demonstrated that hadrons are composed of quarks.

Fermi and Yang had earlier hypothesised that nucleon-antinucleon ($N\overline{N}$ pairs make up all elementary particles. The Fermi-Yang model, however, has the drawback of being unable to produce strange particles from the combination of ($N\overline{N}$ (N & $\overline{N}$ are non-strange particles). The fundamental triplet was formed up of the proton (p), neutron (n), and lambda (Λ particle in Sakata's 1956 model, which he termed the "Sakata model" to make up for the shortcoming. According to theory, p, n, and Λ make up every elementary particle. The fact that one of the basic components (Λ) led to the incorporation of strange particles. When it came to baryons, a combination like $pn\Lambda$ produced the baryon number $B = 3$, but no such state was found. The

Sakata model described the mesons fairly. The combinations which could give $B = 1$ were $p\bar{n}\Lambda$ and $pn\bar{\Lambda}$. Since $\bar{\Lambda}$ has $S = +1$, So if $pn\bar{\Lambda}$ exists we should have a baryon with $S = +1$. The natural world does not contain such a situation, So, the Sakata model also failed. The quark model was made possible by the Sakata model, notwithstanding its shortcomings. In the quark model, particles with fractional baryon numbers serve as the basic triplet rather than p, n, Λ. Gell-Mann and Zwieg called each object with a baryon number 1/3 as quark. They demonstrated that it was possible to think about the Eightfold Way's octet in terms of combinations of a basic triplet of quarks. Gell-Mann showed in his theory that the eight mesons can be considered as a basis for the complexified adjoint representation of SU(3) i.e., its representation on the 8-dimensional Hilbert space. The triplet was made up of the quark types u, d, and s. The three varieties were referred to be the quarks' three flavors. Thus, the initial three flavors of quarks were named upness, downness, and strangeness. Later, researchers found charmness, topness, and bottomness as three additional flavors. Division algebras are employed in theoretical physics to isomorphically represent physical processes. The largest of the four normed division algebras are the octonions (Dickson, 1919). I-spin is a concept that describes how particles behave when they are rotated in isospace in the SU(3) flavour group, whereas U-spin and V-spin are concepts that describe how particles behave when they go through flavor transformations, which call for a change in the kind of quarks that make up the majority of the particle. The properties of the fundamental triplet octonionic quark representation) and their anti-particles ($\bar{u}, \bar{d}, \bar{s}$ shown in Table-1.

2. $SU(3)$ Symmetry and its Generators (Gell-Mann Matrices):

The U(n) group is composed of all $n \times n$ unitary matrices, obeying the defining properties of a group. The special matrices of the U(n) group are those whose unitary determinants are one (detU = 1), and the group whose elements are these special (S) matrices is called the SU(n) group. If $n = 3$, this is the special unitary group in three dimensions i.e., SU(3) group (Joshi, 2013). The representations of the infinitesimal generators of the special unitary group $SU(3)$ are made using Gell-Mann λ matrices. We have general fundamental triplet as

$$\emptyset = \begin{bmatrix} \emptyset_1 \\ \emptyset_2 \\ \emptyset_3 \end{bmatrix}, \tag{1}$$

which transform as $\emptyset \rightarrow \emptyset\,' = U\emptyset$, where U are unitary matrices of unity determinant and the set of unitary matrices as follows,

$$U(\varphi) = e^{\left(\frac{-i}{2}\varphi_a\lambda_a\right)} \tag{2}$$

where φ_a are the eight parameters of $SU(3)$ group and λ_a are the Gell- Mann traceless matrices of $SU(3)$ group forms the fundamental representation. The $SU(3)$ group has eight generators associated with eight Gell-Mann matrices as follows,

$$G_a = \frac{\lambda_a}{2}, (a = 1,2\dots\dots\dots.8) \tag{3}$$

which satisfy the following commutation relations which provide the Lie algebra of SU(3) group (Pushpa *et al.* 2012)

$$[G_a, G_b] = iF_{abc}G_c, \tag{4}$$

where F αβ γ is the structure constants, which is completely antisymmetric under the interchange of any two indices i.e.

$$F^{123} = +1, F^{123} = F^{678} = \frac{\sqrt{3}}{2},$$

$$F^{147} = F^{165} = F^{246} = F^{257} = F^{354} = F^{367} = \frac{1}{2}$$

The Gell-Mann matrices are as follows:

$$\lambda_1 = \begin{bmatrix} 0 & 1 & 0 \\ 1 & 0 & 0 \\ 0 & 0 & 0 \end{bmatrix}, \lambda_2 = \begin{bmatrix} 0 & -i & 0 \\ i & 0 & 0 \\ 0 & 0 & 0 \end{bmatrix}, \lambda_3 = \begin{bmatrix} 1 & 0 & 0 \\ 0 & -1 & 0 \\ 0 & 0 & 0 \end{bmatrix},$$

$$\lambda_4 = \begin{bmatrix} 0 & 0 & 1 \\ 0 & 0 & 0 \\ 1 & 0 & 0 \end{bmatrix}, \lambda_5 = \begin{bmatrix} 0 & 1 & -i \\ 0 & 0 & 0 \\ i & 0 & 0 \end{bmatrix}, \lambda_6 = \begin{bmatrix} 0 & 0 & 0 \\ 0 & 0 & 1 \\ 0 & 1 & 0 \end{bmatrix},$$

$$\lambda_7 = \begin{bmatrix} 0 & 0 & 0 \\ 0 & 0 & -i \\ 0 & i & 0 \end{bmatrix}, \lambda_8 = \frac{1}{\sqrt{3}}\begin{bmatrix} 1 & 0 & 0 \\ 0 & 1 & 0 \\ 0 & 0 & -2 \end{bmatrix}, \tag{5}$$

It satisfies some properties,

$$(\lambda_A)^\dagger = \lambda_A, \tag{6}$$

$$Tr(\lambda_A) = 0, Tr(\lambda_A\lambda_B) = 2\delta_{AB}$$

$$[\lambda_A, \lambda_B] = 2iF_{ABC}\lambda_C, (\forall A, B, C = 1, 2, \ldots\ldots\ldots\ldots\ldots\ldots 8) \qquad\qquad (7)$$

where F_{ABC} is anti-symmetric under interchange of any two indices.

3. Quark Structure of Hadrons:

The reduction of the product of fundamental representation and its conjugate for $SU(3)$ is $3 \times \overline{3} = 8 + 1$, the physical meaning of $3 \times \overline{3}$ is combination of an SU(3) triplet and anti-triplet leading to a singlet and an octet. It constitutes mesons in which eight states transform themselves hence an octet, but do not mix with the ninth (i.e., singlet state). The baryons can be constructed from $3 \times 3 \times 3 = 1 \oplus 8 \oplus 8 \oplus 10$, where two are octets, one is symmetric and other is antisymmetric, it constitutes baryons particle. The combination of a quark and an anti-quark ($q\overline{q}$), and (qqq) can produce a real observable particle. The weight diagrams of quarks and antiquarks are used as a tool in this process. The positions of the three quarks (u, d, and s) are gradually superimposed with the centre of symmetry of the weight diagram of the anti-quarks, and the positions of the anti-quarks ($\overline{u}, \overline{d}$, and $\overline{s}$) are marked in each instance in the $Y - I_3$ plane. It is convenient to classify many of the hadrons (strongly interacting particles) that have been seen so far as belonging to the SU(3) multiplet. Although not all members of the multiplets are thought to have been observed experimentally, they are thought to include the unclassified hadrons. It appears reasonable to expect that many of the known states that are currently unclassified will eventually be found to fit in the hexagonal scheme as new hadrons are continually being discovered. Two additive quantum numbers, the third isospin component (I_3) and the hypercharge Y, gives the characteristics of SU(3).

We already know that a lot of baryons and mesons (also known as hadrons) were created by the intense beams used in current particle accelerators. However, it was impossible to arrange the hadrons that were being seen in an orderly fashion. Before Mendeleev developed the periodic table of elements, a situation similar to this one occurred. Many elements were known at the time, or about a century ago, but there was no systematic way to arrange them. Finally, they were grouped into a periodic table, where the characteristics of the elements served as the foundation for determining where they belonged. In order to place the already found baryons and mesons and make predictions about new ones, an ordered arrangement was necessary here in particle physics (Lee, 2021). The Eightfold Way is a method of arranging baryons and mesons that Murray Gell-Mann introduced in 1961. According to their charge and strangeness (hypercharge), the baryons and mesons are arranged in geometrical patterns by the Eightfold

Way. In particle physics, the Eightfold Way stands in for the Modern Era. The SU(3)-flavor model (as it is currently known) swiftly replaced the Eightfold Way in 1964. We review these models, investigate the eightfold way model's history, and attempt to determine how it relates to the SU(3)-flavor model. The discovery that there was a systematic parallelism between baryons and mesons when one added a new quantum number termed the hypercharge Y to the isospin number provided the origin for the eightfold way model.

3.1. Eightfold Way for Baryon Octet: The two baryons at the center of a hexagonal array made up of the eight lightest baryons fits well. It is also noted that particles with similar charges tend to align themselves along the diagonals denoted by the $Q = +1, Q = 0$ and $Q = -1$ axes. According to the hexagonal pattern, the eight baryons may be various states of a single entity, just as the proton and neutron are two states of the nucleon(N), $\Sigma^{\pm 0}$ are three states of a single entity, and so on. However, the members of N and Σ, etc. are distinguished by a single parameter I_3, whereas the members of the octet are distinguished by two values I_3 and Y. An isospin triplet or doublet's mass discrepancies between its two charge states are a result of electromagnetic self-energy effects brought on by virtual interactions with the electromagnetic field.

However, the breakdown of SU(3) flavour symmetry is thought to be the reason of the large mass difference in the case of the baryon octet, where the difference in mass between the lightest and heaviest member is as large as 379 MeV/C^2. The existence of a significant mass difference also suggests an approximation of the SU(3) flavour symmetry (Bernabeu, 2020). The masses needed to be exactly identical for exact symmetry. Therefore, we can think of the baryons in the octet as distinct states of a single entity due to the approximate nature of SU(3) flavour symmetry.

3.2. Eightfold Way for Meson Octet: Mesons can also be organised in hexagonal patterns, in addition to baryons. The distinction is that, unlike mesons, which are grouped in a specific geometric pattern (a hexagon), baryons and their antiparticles are arranged in different geometric patterns. It should be remembered that in the baryon octet (hexagon), there are no antibaryons and all particles are baryons. Σ^- is not the antiparticle of Σ^+. Thus, we can say that the antiparticles of $\Sigma^{+},\Sigma^{0},\Sigma^{-}$ are and $\overline{\Sigma}^{+},\overline{\Sigma}^{0}$ and $\overline{\Sigma}^{-}$ respectively. Similar to baryon octet, For the smallest pseudoscalar (spin J = 0, parity P = negative) mesons, the Eightfold Way provides a hexagon, but we have three mesons in the centre of the octet. The meson hexagon is hence known as a nonet due to its nine particles.

4. Connection between Octonion and SU(3) Symmetry:

According to the Hurwitz theorem (Cohn, 1973), octonions are the largest normed division algebra over the real numbers and which have eight dimensions (Caley, 1845). It is a non-associative and non-commutative. It can be expressed as

$$O = e_0 O_0 + \sum_{A=1}^{7} e_A O_0 \tag{8}$$

It satisfies some multiplication rules:

$$e_0 = 1, e_0 e_A = e_A e_0 = e_A, e_A^2 = -1,$$

$$e_A e_B = -\delta_{AB} e_0 + f_{ABC} e_C, (A, B.C = 1,2, \dots \dots 7)$$

$$[e_A, e_B] = 2 f_{ABC} e_C, \{e_A, e_B\} = -2\delta_{AB} e_0,$$

$$e_A(e_B e_C) \neq (e_A e_B) e_C. \tag{9}$$

where δ_{AB} is the standard Kronecker delta symbol and f_{ABC} is the Levi Civita three index symbol. The value of f_{ABC} is completely antisymmetric and takes equal to 1 for combinations, (ABC) = (123), (471), (257), (165), (624), (543), (736). The generators of SU(3) group has been connected to octonion in eight dimensions. The SU(3) group of the octonionic Hilbert space has the intrinsic covariance group G_2. So, the SU(3) group is an automorphism of the octonion algebra. The relationship between octonions basis elements (e_j for j = 0 to 7) and Gell-Mann λ_a–matrices can be expressed as (Chanyal, 2021)

$$e_1 \rightarrow i\lambda_1, e_2 \rightarrow i\lambda_2, e_3 \rightarrow i\lambda_3, \quad e_4 = \frac{i}{2}\lambda_4, e_5 = \frac{i}{2}\lambda_5,$$

$$e_6 = \frac{-i}{2}\lambda_6, \quad e_7 = \frac{-i}{2}\lambda_7, e_0 = \frac{\sqrt{3}}{2}\lambda_8, \tag{10}$$

The new elements will still be traceless, which is precisely the property of the Lie algebra of SL(3, C), even though they won't necessarily be anti-hermitian when describing the complexified SU(3) group, the complex linear combinations of the SU(3) elements. Therefore, in octonion representation, the basis of the SL(3, C)–group i.e., $\{E^{12}, E^{23}, E^{13}, E^{21}, E^{32}\ E^{31},\}$ will be equivalent to octonion operators as,

$$u_{12} \rightarrowtail E^{12} = \begin{bmatrix} 0 & 1 & 0 \\ 0 & 0 & 0 \\ 0 & 0 & 0 \end{bmatrix}, \quad u_{45} \rightarrowtail E^{23} = \begin{bmatrix} 0 & 0 & 0 \\ 0 & 0 & 1 \\ 0 & 0 & 0 \end{bmatrix}, \quad u_{67} \rightarrowtail E^{13} = \begin{bmatrix} 0 & 0 & 1 \\ 0 & 0 & 0 \\ 0 & 0 & 0 \end{bmatrix},$$

The conjugate of the above octonionic operators are given as below:

$$\overline{u}_{12} \rightarrowtail E^{21} = \begin{bmatrix} 0 & 0 & 0 \\ 1 & 0 & 0 \\ 0 & 0 & 0 \end{bmatrix}, \quad \overline{u}_{45} \rightarrowtail E^{32} = \begin{bmatrix} 0 & 0 & 0 \\ 0 & 0 & 0 \\ 0 & 1 & 0 \end{bmatrix}, \quad \overline{u}_{67} \rightarrowtail E^{31} = \begin{bmatrix} 0 & 0 & 0 \\ 0 & 0 & 0 \\ 1 & 0 & 0 \end{bmatrix},$$

The octonion complexified multiplets O_j for j = 1, 2, 3, can be represented as,

$$u_{12} = \frac{-i}{2}(e_1 + ie_2), \overline{u}_{12} = \frac{-i}{2}(e_1 - ie_2),$$

$$u_{45} = -i(e_4 + ie_5), \overline{u}_{45} = -i(e_4 - ie_5),$$

$$u_{67} = i(e_6 + ie_7), \overline{u}_{67} = i(e_6 - ie_7), \tag{11}$$

where $\{, \overline{u}_{12}, \left(u_{45}, \overline{u}_{45}\right), \left(u_{67}, \overline{u}_{67}\right)\}$ is the set of complexified octonion shift operators in terms of SU(3) Lie algebra. The three sets of complex octonion operators, however, can only be used to define the I–spin (O_1 –space), V–spin (O_2 –space), and U–spin space) flavor particles in the SU(2)–isospin algebra. Each set of these complexified octonion algebras is isomorphic to the SU(2) isospin algebra. The three sets of octonion isospin multiplets are arranged at an angle of 2/3 degrees in a complexified octonion space. The Cartan generators ($H_1 u_3, H_2 u_0$ corresponding to O_j multiplets can be expressed as

$$u_3^I \rightarrowtail \frac{1}{2}H_1^I = \frac{1}{2}\begin{bmatrix} 1 & 0 & 0 \\ 0 & -1 & 0 \\ 0 & 0 & 0 \end{bmatrix}, u_0^I \rightarrowtail \frac{1}{3}H_2^I = \frac{1}{3}\begin{bmatrix} 1 & 0 & 0 \\ 0 & 1 & 0 \\ 0 & 0 & -2 \end{bmatrix},$$

$$u_3^V \rightarrowtail \frac{1}{2}H_1^V = \frac{1}{2}\begin{bmatrix} -1 & 0 & 0 \\ 0 & 0 & 0 \\ 0 & 0 & 1 \end{bmatrix}, u_0^V \rightarrowtail \frac{1}{3}H_2^V = \frac{1}{3}\begin{bmatrix} 1 & 0 & 0 \\ 0 & -2 & 0 \\ 0 & 0 & 1 \end{bmatrix},$$

$$u_3^U \rightarrowtail \frac{1}{2}H_1^U = \frac{1}{2}\begin{bmatrix} 0 & 0 & 0 \\ 0 & 1 & 0 \\ 0 & 0 & -1 \end{bmatrix}, u_0^U \rightarrowtail \frac{1}{3}H_2^U = \frac{1}{3}\begin{bmatrix} -2 & 0 & 0 \\ 0 & 1 & 0 \\ 0 & 0 & 1 \end{bmatrix}, \tag{12}$$

where $(u|3^I, u_0^I), (u_3^U, u_0^U), \wedge (u_3^V, u_0^V)$ are octonionic Cartan generator in I, U, and V-spin.

5. Octonion Quarks Flavor Symmetry:

The three flavour quarks (up, down, and strange) are necessary in the SU(3) approximation symmetry to explain the known particles like mesons and baryons in Standard Model. Therefore, the three-dimensional vector space in a two-dimensional root system of SU(3)$_f$ symmetry's with their approximate masses will be referred to as

$$u = \begin{pmatrix} 1 \\ 0 \\ 0 \end{pmatrix}, d = \begin{pmatrix} 0 \\ 1 \\ 0 \end{pmatrix}, s = \begin{pmatrix} 0 \\ 0 \\ 1 \end{pmatrix}, \tag{13}$$

and the laws of physics are approximately invariant under applying the unitary transformation to this space (called a flavor rotation), the flavor rotation is only approximate symmetry because the three quarks have different masses. We can therefore examine how complex-octonion space symmetry is associated with the SL(3, C) group (Hall, 2013) and the SU(3)$_f$ symmetry group. One can resemble the three complex-octonion frames in terms of a two-dimensional representation known as octonion triplet symmetry in order to test the vector representation, also known as the "spinor state," of flavour quarks (u, d, and s), and anti-flavor quarks ($\bar{u}, \bar{d}$, and $\bar{s}$), for SU(3)$_f$ symmetry in complex-octonion space (Neill, 2021). If a flavor quark's state vector is ψ_f with weight m which satisfies the octonion eigenvalue equation $u^f_{3,0}\psi_f = m\psi_f$. We may therefore list the octonionic spinor representation of SU(3)$_f$ quarks using the eigenvalue equation (see Table 1), where the octonionic weight of flavor quarks can be shown in terms of (u^I_3, u^I_0), (u^U_3, u^U_0) and (u^V_3, u^V_0) −frames.

Table-1: For Vector Representation Of SU(3) Quarks Flavor In Octonion Frame.

Wt. for (u^I_3, u^I_0)	Spinor rep. for (u^I_3, u^I_0)	Wt. for (u^U_3, u^U_0)	Spinor rep. for (u^U_3, u^U_0)	Wt. for (u^V_3, u^V_0)	Spinor rep. for (u^V_3, u^V_0)	flavor quarks
$\left(\frac{1}{2}, \frac{1}{3}\right)$	$|\nearrow\rangle^I$	$\left(0, -\frac{2}{3}\right)$	$|\downarrow\rangle^U$	$\left(\frac{-1}{2}, \frac{1}{3}\right)$	$|\nwarrow\rangle^V$	u
$\left(\frac{-1}{2}, \frac{1}{3}\right)$	$|\nwarrow\rangle^I$	$\left(\frac{1}{2}, \frac{1}{3}\right)$	$|\nearrow\rangle^U$	$\left(0, -\frac{2}{3}\right)$	$|\downarrow\rangle^V$	d
$\left(0, -\frac{2}{3}\right)$	$|\downarrow\rangle^I$	$\left(\frac{-1}{2}, \frac{1}{3}\right)$	$|\nwarrow\rangle^U$	$\left(\frac{1}{2}, \frac{1}{3}\right)$	$|\nearrow\rangle^V$	s
$\left(\frac{-1}{2}, -\frac{1}{3}\right)$	$|\swarrow\rangle^I$	$\left(0, \frac{2}{3}\right)$	$|\uparrow\rangle^U$	$\left(\frac{1}{2}, -\frac{1}{3}\right)$	$|\searrow\rangle^V$	$\bar{u}$
$\left(\frac{1}{2}, -\frac{1}{3}\right)$	$|\searrow\rangle^I$	$\left(\frac{-1}{2}, -\frac{1}{3}\right)$	$|\swarrow\rangle^U$	$\left(0, \frac{2}{3}\right)$	$|\uparrow\rangle^V$	$\bar{d}$
$\left(0, \frac{2}{3}\right)$	$|\uparrow\rangle^I$	$\left(\frac{1}{2}, -\frac{1}{3}\right)$	$|\searrow\rangle^U$	$\left(\frac{-1}{2}, -\frac{1}{3}\right)$	$|\swarrow\rangle^V$	$\bar{s}$

Hence, the three complexified octonionic isospin spaces are the spinning spaces for SU(3)$_f$ symmetry. Now we can show how the flavour quark and antiquark states exhibit rotational symmetry.

6. Octonion Representation of Eightfold Way for Baryons and Mesons:

The main goal of this section is to explain how complexified octonion space-symmetry can be used to express subatomic particles made up of fundamental flavour quarks. Therefore, we must use an octonionic octet to arrange particles in a hexagonal arrangement in order to indicate the weight of eight baryonic and eight mesonic particles in an octonionic eight-dimensional structure. Octonionic octet is an organisational algebra-based system for a class of subatomic particles that resulted in three suggested complex-octonion spaces. We have drawn the diagram to represent the octonion representation of Eightfold Way for baryons and mesons in three possible complexified octonion isospin frames as shown in figure.

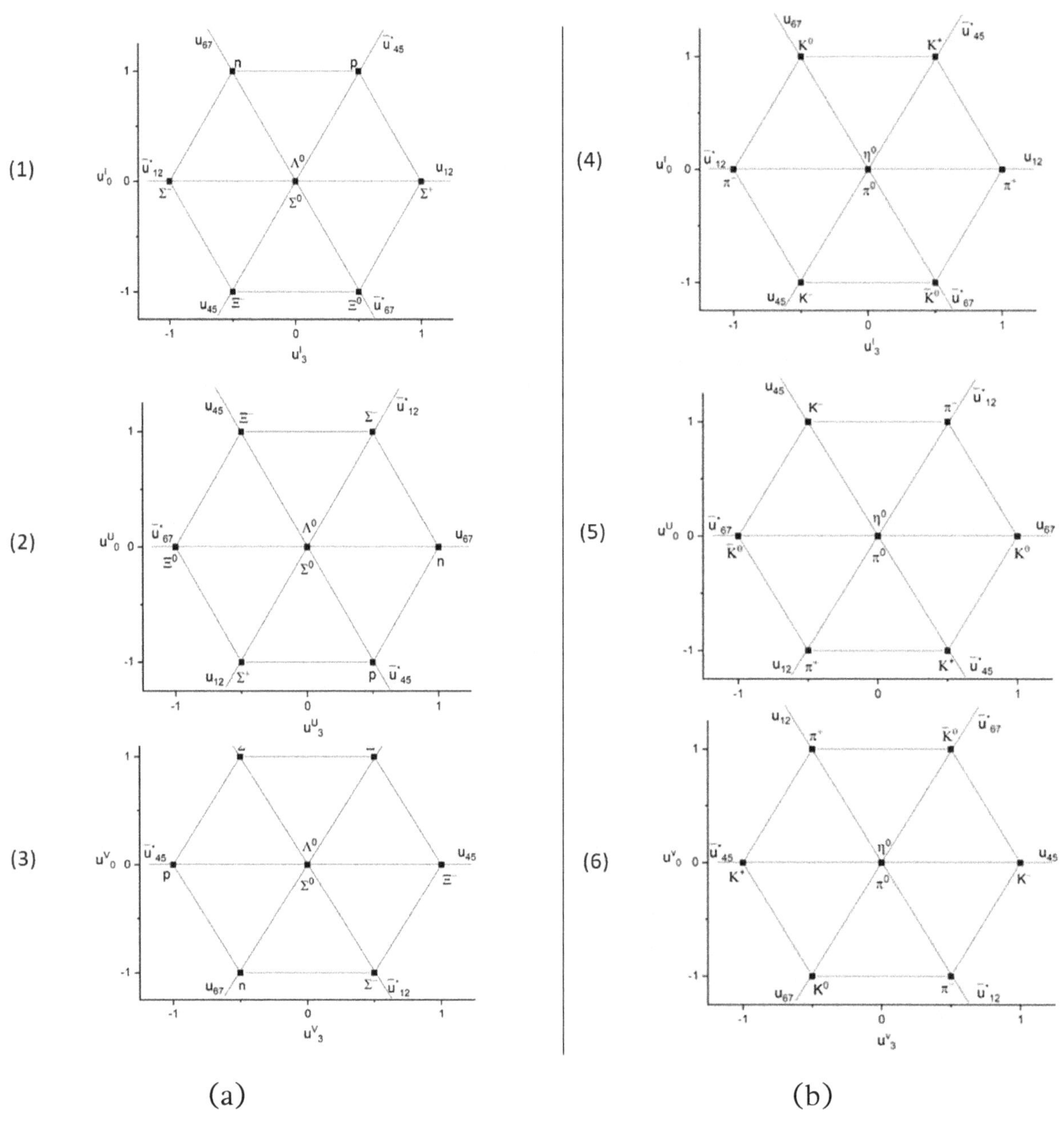

(a)   (b)

Fig.1: Octonion representation of Eightfold Way for baryons and mesons

These are three-dimensional vector space in a two-dimensional root system of $SU(3)_f$ symmetry. We have described the octonion representation of Eightfold Way for baryons and mesons in next two subsections.

6.1. Eightfold Way for Baryon Octet in Octonion frame: In this subsection, we have shown the I, U, V-spinor representation with their octonionic flavor weights, also show the octonion state of baryonic particles (see. Table 2). In this representation, there could be three vector representations of a baryonic state in the complexified octonion state of the SL(3, C) group as shown in given fig. (a). Fig. a (1), a (2), and a (3) shows the octonion representation of baryonic particles in (u_3^I, u_0^I), (u_3^U, u_0^U), and (u_3^V, u_0^V) −frames.

Table 2: For Octonion Representation Of Baryonic Particles:

O_1- space	$I-$ spinor Rep.	O_2- space	$U-$ spinor Rep.	O_3-space	$V-$ spinor Rep.	quark comp.	Sub. Part.	Octonion states
$(1,0)$	$\nearrow\nearrow\downarrow\rangle$	$\left(\frac{-1}{2},-1\right)$	$\downarrow\downarrow\nwarrow\rangle$	$\left(\frac{-1}{2},1\right)$	$\nwarrow\nwarrow\nearrow\rangle$	$uus\rangle$	Σ^+	u_{12}
$\left(\frac{-1}{2},-1\right)$	$\downarrow\downarrow\nwarrow\rangle$	$\left(\frac{-1}{2},1\right)$	$\nwarrow\nwarrow\nearrow\rangle$	$(1,0)$	$\nearrow\nearrow\downarrow\rangle$	$ssd\rangle$	Ξ^-	u_{45}
$\left(\frac{-1}{2},1\right)$	$\nwarrow\nwarrow\nearrow\rangle$	$(1,0)$	$\nearrow\nearrow\downarrow\rangle$	$\left(\frac{-1}{2},-1\right)$	$\downarrow\downarrow\nwarrow\rangle$	$ddu\rangle$	n	u_{67}
$(-1,0)$	$\nwarrow\nwarrow\downarrow\rangle$	$\left(\frac{1}{2},1\right)$	$\nearrow\nearrow\nwarrow\rangle$	$\left(\frac{1}{2},-1\right)$	$\downarrow\downarrow\nearrow\rangle$	$dds\rangle$	Σ^-	$\bar{u}_{12}$
$\left(\frac{1}{2},1\right)$	$\nearrow\nearrow\nwarrow\rangle$	$\left(\frac{1}{2},-1\right)$	$\downarrow\downarrow\nearrow\rangle$	$(-1,0)$	$\nwarrow\nwarrow\downarrow\rangle$	$uud\rangle$	p	$\bar{u}_{45}$
$\left(\frac{1}{2},-1\right)$	$\downarrow\downarrow\nearrow\rangle$	$(-1,0)$	$\nwarrow\nwarrow\downarrow\rangle$	$\left(\frac{1}{2},1\right)$	$\nearrow\nearrow\nwarrow\rangle$	$ssu\rangle$	Ξ^0	$\bar{u}_{67}$

The superposition of these three spinor-states reveals a complete particle's state in octonionic space. At the center of baryon octet representation as shown in above figure. The complete particle's state for neutral baryon particles (i.e., Σ^0 , Λ^0) is the superposition of three isospin frames can be expressed by

$$u_{00}\rangle \rightarrowtail |\nearrow\nwarrow\downarrow\rangle^I + |\downarrow\nearrow\nwarrow\rangle^U + |\nwarrow\downarrow\nearrow\rangle^V. \qquad (15)$$

Similarly, other baryon particles can be expressed as superposition of three isospin I, U, V frames. Therefore, the representation of OBO in SL(3, C) offers the three octonionic approximation symmetry for flavor-quark composite particles (i.e., the octonion symmetry of u_3^I −isospin and hypercharge, u_3^U −isospin and total charge, u_3^V −isospin and rotational-hypercharge). For example, the doublet, neutron and proton have same octonionic hypercharge quantum number ($u|0^I = +1$), which follows isospin symmetry with quantum numbers $u_3^I(n) = -1/2$ and $u_3^I(p) = +1/2$. They do not, however, apply to the U- and V-spin symmetries of octonions.

6.2. Eightfold Way for Meson Octet in Octonion Frame: In this section, the triplet octonion symmetry that corresponds to three sets of SU(2) isospin symmetry has been stated. Fig. b (1), b (2), and b (3) shows the octonion representation of mesonic particles in $(u_3^I, u_0^I, (u_3^U, u_0^U,$ and $(u_3^V, u_0^V$ —frames. By superposing the triplet states, we have determined the complete octonion state of particles. We have constructed baryon octet in three octonionic frames, which further demonstrated the importance of the complexified octonion space as shown in given fig. (b). We have shown the I, U, V-spinor representation with the help of octonionic flavor weights, also show the octonion state of baryonic particles (see. Table 3). As a result, the current theoretical model of complexified octonionic interpretation of flavor quarks for the formation of quark composite particles is more pertinent because it offers fresh understandings of the fundamental properties of particles and their interactions, as well as the symmetries governing the universe. Mesons take part in both the weak interaction and the strong interaction since they are made up of quarks. The electromagnetic interaction also involves mesons with net electric charge. No meson is stable, however mesons with lower masses are more stable than those with higher masses, making them simpler to observe and study in particle accelerators or cosmic ray studies.

Table-3 for octonion representation of the mesonic particles:

O_1- space	$I-$ spinor Rep.	O_2- space	$U-$ spinor Rep.	O_3-space	$V-$ spinor Rep.	quark comp.	Sub. Part.	Octonion states
$(1,0)$	$\nearrow\searrow\rangle$	$\left(\frac{-1}{2},-1\right)$	$\downarrow\swarrow\rangle$	$\left(\frac{-1}{2},1\right)$	$\nwarrow\uparrow\rangle$	$u\bar{d}\rangle$	π^+	u_{12}
$\left(\frac{-1}{2},-1\right)$	$\downarrow\swarrow\rangle$	$\left(\frac{-1}{2},1\right)$	$\nwarrow\uparrow\rangle$	$(1,0)$	$\nearrow\searrow\rangle$	$s\bar{u}\rangle$	k^-	u_{45}
$\left(\frac{-1}{2},1\right)$	$\nwarrow\uparrow\rangle$	$(1,0)$	$\nearrow\searrow\rangle$	$\left(\frac{-1}{2},-1\right)$	$\downarrow\swarrow\rangle$	$d\bar{s}\rangle$	k^0	u_{67}
$(-1,0)$	$\nwarrow\swarrow\rangle$	$\left(\frac{1}{2},1\right)$	$\nearrow\uparrow\rangle$	$\left(\frac{1}{2},-1\right)$	$\downarrow\searrow\rangle$	$d\bar{u}\rangle$	π^-	$\bar{u}_{12}$
$\left(\frac{1}{2},1\right)$	$\nearrow\uparrow\rangle$	$\left(\frac{1}{2},-1\right)$	$\downarrow\searrow\rangle$	$(-1,0)$	$\nwarrow\swarrow\rangle$	$u\bar{s}\rangle$	k^+	$\bar{u}_{45}$
$\left(\frac{1}{2},-1\right)$	$\downarrow\searrow\rangle$	$(-1,0)$	$\nwarrow\swarrow\rangle$	$\left(\frac{1}{2},1\right)$	$\nearrow\uparrow\rangle$	$s\bar{d}\rangle$	$\bar{k}^0$	$\bar{u}_{67}$

The superposition of three octonionic spinors can be used to describe the complete spinor state of mesonic particles. Hence, we can see that in mesonic u_3^I-spin symmetry, we can observe the symmetry between particles along with the same u_0^I, we have other flavor symmetries in u_3^U-spin and u_3^V-spin symmetry. As we can see in fig. (a, b), there exist symmetry between some particles. The complete particle's state of , η) is the superposition of three isospin frames can be expressed by

$$u_{00}\rangle \mapsto (|\nearrow\swarrow\rangle - |\nwarrow\searrow\rangle))^I + (|\downarrow\uparrow\rangle - |\nearrow\swarrow\rangle))^U + (|\nwarrow\searrow\rangle - |\downarrow\uparrow\rangle))^V, \qquad (16)$$

$$u_{00}\rangle \mapsto (|\nearrow\swarrow\rangle + |\nwarrow\searrow\rangle - 2|\downarrow\uparrow\rangle))^I + (|\downarrow\uparrow\rangle + |\nearrow\swarrow\rangle - 2|\nwarrow\searrow\rangle))^U + (|\nwarrow\searrow\rangle + |\downarrow\uparrow\rangle - 2|\nearrow\swarrow\rangle))^V, \quad (17)$$

where equation (16) represents the spinor state of neutral meson (π^0 and equation (17) represents the spinor state of η-meson particle in I, U, V-spin symmetry. Similarly, the complete spinor state of other mesonic particles can be expressed by the superposition of three isospin frames in I, U, and V-spin symmetry.

7. Result and Conclusion:

The $SU(3)$ flavor symmetry for quarks and antiquarks have been demonstrated via the complexified octonion space, where the six complex-octonion operators are essentially identical to the SL(3, C) group generators. The three sets of complex octonion-valued operators have been used to describe I, U, and V-spin symmetry in the context of SU(2)-isospin algebra. While U-spin and V-spin symmetry are not the exact symmetries of strong interactions in this context, however, they are the adequate approximation. They nonetheless demonstrate a helpful idea for rotational symmetry. As a result, the complexified octonion space has demonstrated its value in constructing the baryon octet and meson octet in three different isospin frames. The significance of complex octonion space is that a set of three baryons and mesons (π^{+,k^{-},k^0}) are structured along three octonion bases (u_{12}, u_{45}, u_{67}), next set of three baryons and mesons are structured along complex octonion bases ($\bar{u}_{12}^{\square}, \bar{u}_{45}^{\square}, \bar{u}_{67}^{\square}$ while two baryons , Λ^0) and mesons (π^0, η) are kept at the centre of the octet with octonion basis (u_{00}). We have also determined the Gell-Mann-Nishijima relation in terms complex octonion variables, however, it is approximately true for three complexified octonion symmetry. The function of three possible complex-octonionic spinor bases (known as SU(2) isospinors) for SU(3) flavour quarks has been discussed. It has also been shown that a more precise method for calculating the full spinor state of hadrons by the help of octonionic-valued three frames, which usually follow I, U, and V-symmetries. When we express the full eigenfunction of a particle, the spinor state plays a more significant role. Thus, it is claimed that the complexified form of octonions is the extended theory of quark flavours, which maintains the property of non-commutativity. The SU(3) colour symmetry, which is thought to be an exact symmetry, be added to the current theoretical model. In color symmetry, quarks have same mass, so it is an exact symmetry.

8. Refrences:

1. Anishetty, R., Mathur, M. and Raychowdhury, I. (2009). Irreducible SU(3) Schwinger Bosons. *J. Math. Phys.*, 50(5): 053503-053520.

2. Bernabeu, J. (2020). Symmetries and their breaking in the fundamental laws of physics. *Symmetry*, 12(8): 1316-1343.

3. Cayley, A. (1845). On Jacobi's Elliptic functions, in reply to the Rev. Brice Bronwin; and on Quaternions. *Lond. Edinb. Dublin philos. Mag. J. Sci.*, 26(172): 208-211.

4. Chanyal, B. C. (2021). On octonion quark confinement condition. *Mod. Phys. Lett. A.*, 36(37): 2150264-2150277.

5. Cohn, J. H. E. (1973). Hurwitz theorem. *Proc. Amer. Math. Soc.*, 38(2): 436-436.

6. Conversi, M., Pancini, E. and Piccioni, O. 1947. On the disintegration of negative mesons. *Phys. Rev.*, 71(3): 209-210.

7. Dickson L. E. (1919), "On Quaternions and Their Generalization and the History of the Eight Square Theorem", *Ann. Math.*, 20(3): 155-171.

8. Gell-Mann, M. (1964). Elementary Particle Physics. Volume No. 9, Springer, Vienna, Austria. Pp. 733-761.

9. Griffiths, D. J. (1987). Introduction to Particle Physics. Edition No. II. John Wiley & sons, Canada. Pp 301-309.

10. Hall, B. C. (2013). Lie groups, Lie algebras, and representations. In Quantum Theory for Mathematicians. Springer, New York, USA. pp 333-366

11. Joshi, D.C. (2006). Introduction to Quantum Electrodynamics and Particle Physics. I.K. International Publishing House Pvt. Ltd. New Delhi, India. pp 190-191.

12. Lee, H. M. (2021). Lectures on physics beyond the Standard Model. *J. Korean Phys. Soc.*, 78(11): 985-1017.

13. Marshak, R. E. (1988). From two mesons and (VA) weak currents to the standard model of quark and lepton interactions. *Pramana,* 31(1): pp 9-39.

14. Neill C. O. (2021), "Octonions, the three flavours of matter and a new kind of super-symmetry", *Can. J. Pure. Appl. Sci.,* 15(2): 5261-5268.

15. Peskin, M. E. and Schroeder, D. V. (1996). An Introduction to Quantum Field Theory, Taylor & Francis, Addison-Wesley, New York. 842 p.

16. Pushpa., Bisht, P. S., Li, T. and Negi, O. P. S. (2012). Quaternion-Octonion SU(3) Flavour Symmetry. *Int. J. Theor. Phys.,* 51(6): 1866-1875.

17. Weinberg, S. (1995). The quantum theory of fields (Vol. 2). Cambridge University Press, Cambridge, England. 233 p.

11. Green Chemistry Principle in Various Industrial Process

Laxmi Narayan Suthar

Research Scholar, Department of Chemistry, Bikaner Technical University, Bikaner
(Rajasthan), 334001)
Email: laxminarayan007@gmail.com

Abstract:

Green chemistry is the design of chemical products and processes that reduce or eliminate the use or generation of hazardous substances. Green chemistry applies across the life cycle of a chemical product, including its design, manufacture, use, and ultimate disposal. It investigates various strategies, case studies, and challenges associated with adopting green chemistry practices in different industries. Green chemistry is commonly used in the chemical, pharmaceutical, paper, polymer, clothing, and color industries. It is also important in various energy sciences and the development of novel techniques for producing solar cells, fuel cells, and batteries for energy storage.
Keywords: Green Chemistry, Sustainablity, Environmnet, Economy

1. Introduction

The word sustainability refers to the ability to provide a healthy and satisfying life for all people on mother earth, now and for generation to come, while enhancing the health of ecosystem and the ability of other species to survive in their natural environment. In 1987 a United Nation report defined sustainable development as needs. This report is often recognized as the genesis of the modern sustainability movement. As the challenges of living in harmony with the earth becomes increasingly difficult, more than ever, society needs education and high-quality cutting-edge research to meet this challenge (Matlin et al., 2015). "Development that meets the needs of present without compromising the ability of future generation to meet their own. In the recent years, Green Chemistry has gained a strong foothold in the areas of research and development in both industry and academia, especially in the developed industrial countries. Green chemistry has to cover a broad section of chemical and technological aspects in order to offer its alternative vision for sustainable development (Tundo et al., 2000). Green Chemistry had to include fundamental ways to reduce or to eliminate environmental pollution through dedicated sustainable prevention programs. Green chemistry must focus on alternative environment friendly chemicals in synthetic routes but also to increase reaction rates and lower reaction temperature to save energy. Green Chemistry looks very carefully on reaction efficiency, use of less toxic solvents, minimizing the hazards of feedstocks and products and reduction of waste. Father of green chemistry is 'Paul Anastas'.

2. Principles of Green Chemistry:

The 12 principles of green chemistry, formulated by Paul Anastas and John Warner, provide a framework for designing chemical processes and products that minimize environmental impact (Anastas and Beach, 2007). Here they are, along with examples of how each principle can be applied in industrial processes:

2.1. **Prevention**: It is better to prevent waste than to treat or clean up waste after it is formed. Example: Using catalytic processes to minimize the formation of unwanted by-products in chemical reactions, thus reducing waste generation.

2.2. **Atom Economy**: The goal is to maximize the incorporation of all materials used in the process into the final product. This principle promotes efficiency and minimizes the generation of by-products Synthetic methods should be designed to maximize the incorporation of all materials used in the process into the final product.
Example: Designing synthesis routes that maximize the utilization of starting materials and minimize the formation of by-products.

2.3. **Less Hazardous Chemical Syntheses**: Wherever possible, synthetic methods should be designed to use and generate substances that possess little to no toxicity to human health and the environment.
Example: Developing greener solvents and reagents that are less toxic and more environmentally benign.

2.4. **Designing Safer Chemicals**: Chemical products should be designed to be effective while minimizing toxicity.
Example: Designing pharmaceuticals with improved efficacy and reduced toxicity profiles through structure-activity relationship studies.

2.5. **Safer Solvents and Auxiliaries**: The use of auxiliary substances (e.g., solvents, separation agents) should be made unnecessary wherever possible and innocuous when used.

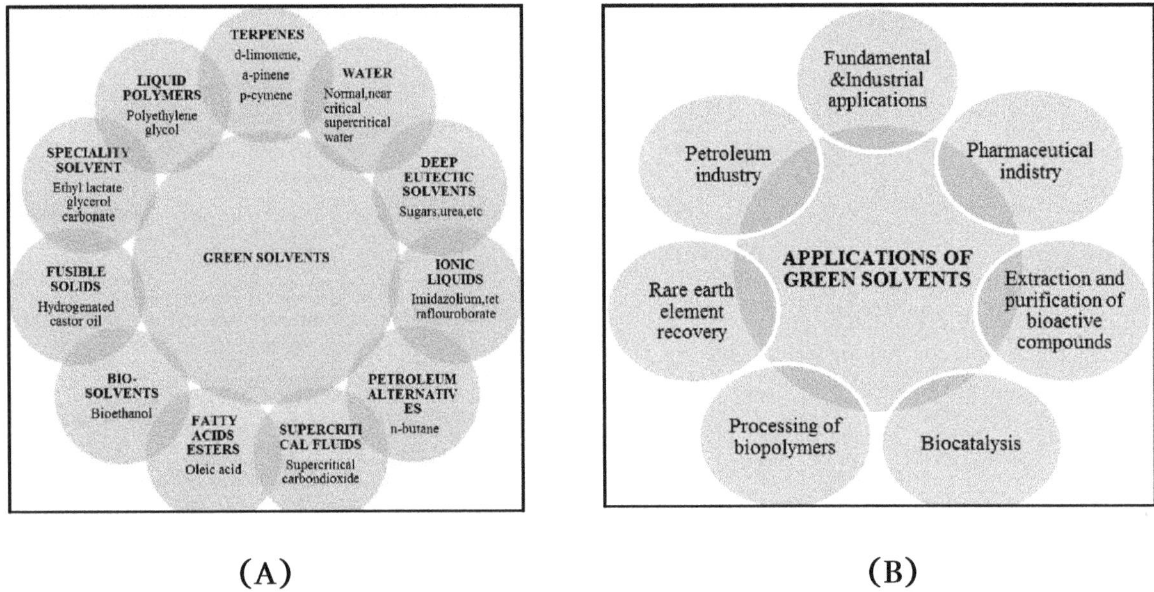

(A)   (B)

Figure 1: (A) Green Solvents (B) Applications of Green Solvents

2.6. Design for Energy Efficiency: Energy requirements of chemical processes should be minimized to reduce consumption and environmental impact.

Example: Implementing energy-efficient reaction conditions, such as using microwave or ultrasound irradiation, or optimizing reaction temperatures.

2.7. Use of Renewable Feedstocks: Whenever practicable, raw materials should be renewable rather than depleting.

Example: Utilizing biomass-derived feedstocks instead of fossil fuels for the production of fuels, chemicals, and materials.

2.8. Reduce Derivatives: Unnecessary derivatization (use of blocking groups, protection/deprotection, temporary modification of physical/chemical processes) should be minimized or avoided if possible because such steps require additional reagents and can generate waste.

Example: Designing synthetic routes that minimize the need for protection and deprotection steps in organic synthesis.

2.9. Catalysis: Catalytic reagents are superior to stoichiometric reagents.

Example: Employing catalytic processes to promote specific transformations with higher efficiency and selectivity, reducing the need for stoichiometric reagents and generating less waste.

2.10. **Design for Degradation**: Chemical products should be designed so that at the end of their function they do not persist in the environment and instead break down into innocuous degradation products.

Example: Designing biodegradable polymers that can be easily degraded by environmental processes after their useful life.

2.11. **Real-Time Analysis for Pollution Prevention**: Analytical methodologies need to be further developed to allow for real-time, in-process monitoring and control prior to the formation of hazardous substances.

Example: Implementing online monitoring techniques such as spectroscopy or chromatography to detect and control impurities and by-products during chemical processes.

2.12. **Inherently Safer Chemistry for Accident Prevention**: Substances and the form of a substance used in a chemical process should be chosen to minimize the potential for chemical accidents, including releases, explosions, and fires.

Example: Selecting inherently safer reaction pathways and process conditions to mitigate the risks associated with hazardous materials and reactions.

3. Green Chemistry Principle Use Different Type of Industry Like:

Green chemistry principles can be applied across various industries to promote sustainability and reduce environmental impact. Here are some examples of how different industries utilize green chemistry principles:

3.1. **Pharmaceutical Industry**: In pharmaceutical industry green chemistry plays an important role and makes a revolution in it. BASF, a chemical company now makes ibuprofen (painkiller) in a three-step rather than a six-step process (Grover et al., 2023). Zocor (simvastatin), leading drug for treating high cholesterol, conventionally synthesized using a multistep method concerning huge quantities of hazardous reagents that formed a big amount of toxic waste. A bio-catalysis company, Codexis developed a new technique for synthesizing the drug using an engineered enzyme and a low-cost feedstock. The chemotherapy drug paclitaxel (marketed as Taxol) was made by takeout from yew tree bark, a process that used a large amount of solvent for killing the tree. The drug is now made by growing tree cells in a fermentation vat (Cechinel-Filho, 2012).

3.2. Agrochemical Industry: The agricultural industry has witnessed a transformation with green chemistry practices. Green chemistry enables the production of eco-friendly pesticides, herbicides, and fertilizers. Sustainable pesticides, fertilizers, and crop protection methods are being developed to minimize soil and water contamination while ensuring high crop yields. These developments play a pivotal role in maintaining ecological balance and promoting food security (Ameta and Ameta, 2021).

3.3. Textile Industry: Green chemistry emerged as an effective and advantageous tool to make textile processing sustainable and also helped in the development of **alternative** green and biodegradable chemicals useable as wetting, washing, and finishing agents (Gulzar et al., 2019). Green chemistry is essentially a branch of chemistry that reduces any adverse environmental impact of chemical processes and products for sustainable development and provides a solution for many health and environmental economic problems caused by industrial chemicals. This chapter deals with the review of new approaches and techniques of green chemistry implemented for the development of the textile industry. Eco-Friendly Dry clean-up of Clothes Per chloro ethylene (PERC) used for dry cleaning pollutes water and cancer-causing agent. To solve this problem, now a days super critical CO_2 and a surfactant for cleaning garments was first developed by Joseph De Simons, Timothy Romark, and James. Micell Technology has likewise developed a metal cleaning framework that utilize CO_2 and a surfactant accordingly replacing halogenated solvents.

3.4. Biodegradable Eco-friendly Packaging Materials: In the 20th century, change in the global climate was identified as one of the most serious issues that the world faces. The main reason for this problem is high consumptions of fossil fuel which represent about 80% of the global energy usage. The combustion of fossil fuel results in the emission of greenhouse gases especially CO_2. There are several techniques that are used to capture CO_2 such as adsorbing by chemicals like amines, carbonates, ammonia or by pre-combustion techniques such as chemical looping combustion processes. However, these techniques are insufficient to suppress the rapid increase in the environmental CO_2 concentration resulting from fossil fuel combustion. Also, the high demands of fossil fuel lead to another problem which is a severe depletion of this important source of energy. Although, there are several ways to create clean energy from the wind, the sun and water, the use of biomass is very important because unlike the other energy sources it provides liquid fuel for transportation. The United States is at the forefront of the bio fuel market with a target of substituting 20% of the transportation fossil fuel with biofuel.

Formulating packaging materials with non-toxic and biodegradable polymers, such as polylactic acid (PLA) and polyhydroxyalkanoates (PHAs), to reduce environmental impact (Naser et al., 2021). Green chemistry promotes the use of renewable feedstocks, such as plant-based biomass, for the production of biodegradable packaging materials, reducing dependence on fossil fuels. Developing packaging materials that degrade readily in various environments, including compostable and marine-degradable options, to minimize pollution and waste accumulation. Green chemistry principles encourage the synthesis of packaging materials with high atom economy to minimize the use of raw materials and reduce waste generation during production.

3.5. Development of Biofuels: Green chemistry principles emphasize utilizing renewable resources as feedstocks for biofuel production, such as agricultural residues, algae, and waste oils (Pfaltzgraff and Clark, 2014). Efficient conversion of biomass into biofuels while minimizing energy consumption and waste generation. Green chemistry encourages the development of energy-efficient processes for biofuel production, such as enzymatic hydrolysis and fermentation, which require less energy input compared to traditional methods. Processes with high atom economy are favored to minimize waste generation during biofuel synthesis, ensuring that the maximum amount of starting material is converted into useful products. Depending upon the feedstock, biofuels are categorized into four as follow:

> *First Generation:* Biofuels are obtained from edible biomass such as sugarcane, corn, wheat grains, oil seeds, vegetable oils and renders animal fats. They are also known as conventional biofuels such as ethanol prepared by fermentation of sugarcane or sugar beds. Most commonly known first generation biofuels are biogas, biodiesel and bio alcohol. The future success of first-generation biofuel is limited as it negatively impacts greenhouse gas emissions, biodiversity, land use and water use due to increase use of fertilizers to grow crops for biofuels, which has led to increased amounts of nitrogen and phosphorus entering ground and surface water. These biofuels are likely to be banned in European Union to secure the food supply as the compromise to edible food stocks.

> *Second Generation:* Biofuels are derived from cellulosic biomass sources including crop residues, perennial grasses and trees. They may be grown on marginal cropland where crop production is not profitable. By focusing on areas that are highly erodible or have marginal soil quality, this avoid competition with fertile ground that may be best used to grow food crops. Although this crop required little initial input, they do require

additional treatment to break down cellulose for creating an end product such as liquid fuel. In addition, transporting high quantities of biomass can be a logistical and financial challenge for production, all such things make reasons for limiting the second biofuels.

➢ *Third Generation:* Recently researchers have focused their interest on the algal biomass as an alternative feed stock for the production of biofuels. Moreover, algal biomass has no competition with agriculture food and feed production. The photosynthetic microorganisms like microalgae require mainly light, carbon dioxide and some nutrients (nitrogen, phosphorus and potassium) for its growth and to produce large amount of lipids and carbohydrates, which can be further processed into different biofuels and other valuable co-products. There are several advantages of algal biomass for biofuel production such as

(a) Ability to grow throughout the year

(b) Higher tolerance of high CO_2 content

(c) The consumptions rate of water is very less in algal cultivation

(d) No requirement of herbicides and pesticides

(e) Growth potential of algal species is very high and

(f) Ability to grow under harsh condition like saline brackish water, coastal sea water where other cultivation is not possible.

➢ *Fourth Generation:* While microbial biofuel production is a well-established practice in a small-scale system, its industrial scale production is not economically viable. This is mainly due to the low lipid content and growth rate of microbial strain. Genetic engineers offer a wide range of options to enhance the lack of industrial competent strains by several approaches such as transcription and targeted expression of key proteins involved in microalgal lipogenesis. Production of biofuels from genetically engineered algae have been discussed by scientist in FGB terms. The FGB- photo logical solar fuel and electro fuels are expected to bring fundamental breakthrough in the field of biofuel. Technology for production of such solar fuel is an emerging field and based on direct conversion of solar energy into fuel using raw material that are inexhaustible, cheap and widely available .

3.6. Waste Management: Green chemistry emphasizes waste prevention through the adoption of cleaner production techniques and the development of products that generate less waste during their lifecycle. Catalytic processes are utilized in waste management to facilitate the conversion of waste materials into valuable products or energy sources through processes such as catalytic depolymerization and gasification. Developing biodegradable materials and products to reduce the accumulation of persistent waste in landfills and the environment. Green chemistry promotes the use of safer alternatives in waste treatment processes to minimize environmental contamination and health risks associated with hazardous chemicals (Chen et al., 2020).

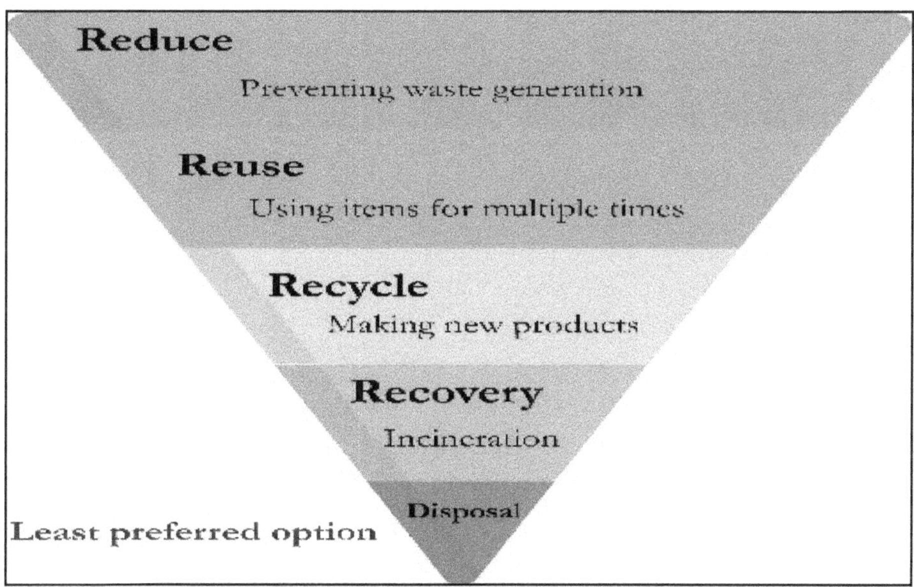

Figure 1: Waste Management System

3.7. Food Industry: Using renewable agricultural feedstocks for food processing and packaging materials. Implementing energy-efficient processes for food preservation and processing to reduce energy consumption. Preventing food waste through improved packaging materials and preservation techniques to extend shelf life.

3.8. Automotive Industry: Developing lightweight materials and energy-efficient manufacturing processes to reduce fuel consumption and emissions. Using catalytic converters to reduce emissions of harmful pollutants from automotive exhaust gases. Designing recycling processes for end-of-life vehicles to maximize the recovery of valuable materials and minimize waste generation.

3.9. Cosmetics Industry: Formulating cosmetics with ingredients that have lower toxicity and allergenicity profiles. Using natural and biodegradable solvents in cosmetic formulations to reduce environmental impact. Developing biodegradable microbeads and packaging materials to reduce plastic pollution in the environment.

4. Benefits of Green Chemistry in Industry

4.1. Human health:

- Cleaner air: Less release of hazardous chemicals to air leading to less damage to lungs
- Cleaner water: less release of hazardous chemical wastes to water leading to cleaner drinking and recreational water
- Increased safety for workers in the chemical industry; less use of toxic materials; less personal protective equipment required; less potential for accidents (e.g., fires or explosions)
- Safer consumer products of all types: new, safer products will become available for purchase; some products (e.g., drugs) will be made with less waste; some products (i.e., pesticides, cleaning products) will be replacements for less safe products
- Safer food: elimination of persistent toxic chemicals that can enter the food chain; safer pesticides that are toxic only to specific pests and degrade rapidly after use
- Less exposure to such toxic chemicals as endocrine disruptors

4.2. Environment:

- Many chemicals end up in the environment by intentional release during use (e.g., pesticides), by unintended releases (including emissions during manufacturing), or by disposal. Green chemicals either degrade to innocuous products or are recovered for further use
- Plants and animals suffer less harm from toxic chemicals in the environment
- Lower potential for global warming, ozone depletion, and smog formation
- Less chemical disruption of ecosystems
- Less use of landfills, especially hazardous waste landfills

4.3. Economy and Business:

- Higher yields for chemical reactions, consuming smaller amounts of feedstock to obtain the same amount of product
- Fewer synthetic steps, often allowing faster manufacturing of products, increasing plant capacity, and saving energy and water
- Reduced waste, eliminating costly remediation, hazardous waste disposal, and end-of-the-pipe treatments

- Allow replacement of a purchased feedstock by a waste product
- Better performance so that less product is needed to achieve the same function.

5. Challenges and Barriers

5.1. Initial Cost and Investment: One of the primary challenges in implementing green chemistry practices is the initial cost and investment required to transition from traditional chemical processes to more sustainable alternatives (García-Serna et al., 2017). New technologies, equipment, and research and development efforts can be costly, posing financial constraints for industries, especially smaller businesses.

5.2. Education and Awareness: Another hurdle is the lack of widespread education and awareness about green chemistry principles. Many industries and professionals may be unaware of the potential benefits of adopting green practices, making it crucial to promote and disseminate knowledge about sustainable alternatives.

5.3. Regulatory and Policy Barriers: Navigating regulatory and policy barriers can be daunting for businesses looking to incorporate green chemistry into their operations. Existing regulations may not fully accommodate or incentivize the adoption of sustainable practices, leading to uncertainty and reluctance to change.

5.4. Compatibility with Existing Infrastructure: For well-established industries, integrating green chemistry practices may require significant modifications to existing infrastructure and processes. This can be challenging, particularly for industries that have relied on conventional methods for a long time.

5.5. Scaling Up Sustainable Technologies: While some green chemistry innovations may show promise on a laboratory scale, scaling them up to industrial levels can present technical challenges. Ensuring that sustainable technologies can meet the demands of large-scale production is a crucial aspect that needs to be addressed.

5.6. Mindset Shift: Embracing green chemistry demands a fundamental shift in mindset and corporate culture, as companies need to prioritize sustainability over short-term gains.

6. Microwave Irradiation Approach:

Synthesis procedures using microwave irradiation is an advanced opportunity for synthesis of materials. Microwave radiation is known to have a faster heating rate than the conventional heating through conduction and convection. The microwave radiation heats up a material through its dielectric loss, which converts the radiation energy into thermal energy. The interaction of electric field of a microwave with dipole moment of molecules occurs during microwave heating; thus, polar solvents like water and ionic liquids are the best solvents to use in microwave synthesis. It is used in synthesis of many organic, inorganic, nanomaterials etc (Kumar et al., 2020).

7. Conclusion:

As demonstrated by the aforementioned technological advancements, green chemistry principles have made significant strides over the past decades. Research on various industrial applications has yielded substantial benefits, including reduced energy consumption, the creation of less toxic products, and minimal waste. Green chemistry emphasizes the design and adoption of better synthetic routes that focus on cleaner production techniques, energy-saving methods, and less harmful consumer products. From fuels, pesticides, and fertilizers to elastomers, plastics, medicines, analytical reagents, and other commercial products, major industries are increasingly prioritizing the production of safer, healthier, and more environmentally friendly products. This shift is not merely driven by technological advancements that offer alternative methodologies but also by the economic rationale behind these changes. By participating in the goals of sustainability and environmental protection, industries are not only safeguarding the environment but also ensuring the future availability of essential resources for feedstocks and energy. Thus, the integration of green chemistry principles into industrial practices supports both ecological sustainability and economic viability, paving the way for a healthier planet and a more sustainable future.

References:

1. Matlin, S. A., Mehta, G., Hopf, H., & Krief, A. (2015). The role of chemistry in inventing a sustainable future. *Nature chemistry, 7*(12), 941-943.
2. Tundo, P., Anastas, P., Black, D. S., Breen, J., Collins, T. J., Memoli, S., ... & Tumas, W. (2000). Synthetic pathways and processes in green chemistry. Introductory overview. *Pure and Applied Chemistry, 72*(7), 1207-1228.
3. Abuhijleh, A. L. (1994). Mononuclear and binuclear copper (II) complexes of the antiinflammatory drug ibuprofen: synthesis, characterization, and catecholase-mimetic activity. *Journal of inorganic biochemistry, 55*(4), 255-262.

4. Pfaltzgraff, L. A., & Clark, J. H. (2014). Green chemistry, biorefineries and second generation strategies for re-use of waste: an overview. *Advances in biorefineries*, 3-33.

5. Naser, A. Z., Deiab, I., & Darras, B. M. (2021). Poly (lactic acid)(PLA) and polyhydroxyalkanoates (PHAs), green alternatives to petroleum-based plastics: a review. *RSC advances, 11*(28), 17151-17196.

6. Gulzar, T., Farooq, T., Kiran, S., Ahmad, I., & Hameed, A. (2019). Green chemistry in the wet processing of textiles. In *The impact and prospects of green chemistry for textile technology* (pp. 1-20). Woodhead Publishing.

7. Ameta, S. K., & Ameta, S. C. (2021). Eco-friendly approaches of using weeds for sustainable plant growth and production. *Plant Performance Under Environmental Stress: Hormones, Biostimulants and Sustainable Plant Growth Management*, 559-592.

8. Cechinel-Filho, V. (2012). *Plant bioactives and drug discovery: principles, practice, and perspectives.* John Wiley & Sons.

9. Grover, T., Chauhan, R., Gajjar, A., Dhameliya, T., & Vaja, M. (2023). Impact of Green Approaches in Pharmaceutical Industries. *Sustainable Approaches in Pharmaceutical Sciences*, 65-90.

10. Anastas, P. T., & Beach, E. S. (2007). Green chemistry: the emergence of a transformative framework. *Green Chemistry Letters and Reviews, 1*(1), 9-24.

11. Alalwan, H. A., Alminshid, A. H., & Aljaafari, H. A. (2019). Promising evolution of biofuel generations. Subject review. *Renewable Energy Focus, 28*, 127-139.

12. Garyali, S., Kumar, A., & Reddy, M. S. (2013). Taxol production by an endophytic fungus, Fusarium redolens, isolated from Himalayan yew. *Journal of microbiology and biotechnology, 23*(10), 1372-1380.

13. Chen, T. L., Kim, H., Pan, S. Y., Tseng, P. C., Lin, Y. P., & Chiang, P. C. (2020). Implementation of green chemistry principles in circular economy system towards sustainable development goals: Challenges and perspectives. *Science of the Total Environment, 716*, 136998.

14. García-Serna, J., Pérez-Barrigón, L., & Cocero, M. J. (2007). New trends for design towards sustainability in chemical engineering: Green engineering. *Chemical Engineering Journal, 133*(1-3), 7-30.

15. Kumar, A., Kuang, Y., Liang, Z., & Sun, X. (2020). Microwave chemistry, recent advancements, and eco-friendly microwave-assisted synthesis of nanoarchitectures and their applications: a review. *Materials Today Nano, 11*, 100076.

12. Demonstrating Toximp – The Impact of Microplastics on Soil Ecosystem

Dr. R. Gomathy Sankari[1] and S. Harini Sree[2]

[1]Assistant Professor, Faculty of Law, Dr. Mgr Educational and Research Institute,
Maduoravoyal, Chennai -600095
Email: Rgsankariphd@gmail.com
BBA - LLB (Hons)
[2]Dr. Mgr Educational and Research Institute, Maduoravoyal, Chennai-600095
Email: harinishreesumathi@gmail.com

Abstract:

Microplastics are smaller tiny particles; they are less than 5mm in size. Microplastics are found almosteverywhere, even in oceans, rivers, soil and air which making them a global concern. Marine organisms, including fish and plankton (tiny organism that float in the ocean or in bodies of water) often ingestmicroplastics. This can lead to bioaccumulation, where plastics move into the food chain. It can also absorb andcarry toxic chemicals including POPs (persistent organic pollutants) such as PCBs (polychlorinatedbiphenyls) and pesticides, even heavy metals like mercury and lead. And other harmful substances prevailing in the environment which are later transferred into organisms posing a greater threat to both marine and human life. Microplastics can become airborne through processes like tire wear and breakdown of synthetic textiles, potentially affecting respiratory health when inhaled. In aspects of soil contamination, it can hinder the growth of plants, disrupt soil ecosystem and affect agricultural productivity. This TOXIMP appears to be a blend of Toxicology and Microplastics focusing on the Toxicological aspects of Microplastics. This article mainly examines how these small plastic particles can accumulate toxic chemicals in our Environment.

Keywords: TOXIMP, POPs, PCBs, Soil contamination

1. Introduction:

"Microplastics, defined as plastic particles no larger than 5 millimeters, originate from sources like tire abrasion, textile fiber shedding, pellet production, and paint (Xu et al., 2020). These primary microplastics contaminate the environment, exacerbated by improper waste disposal. Within water bodies, the chemical additives associated with microplastics accumulate, posing significant risks to human health. These additives include heavy metals, polyamidoamine-epichlorohydrins, bisphenol A, brominated flame retardants, and per- and polyfluoroalkyl substances (Chen et al., 2022). Factors such as light, temperature, and coexisting pollutants influence the release of these chemicals, leading to toxicity in animals that ingest them. Some of these additives contribute to neurotoxicity, inflammation, metabolic disorders, and even cancer. They pose a significant threat to both human health and the environment. They enter the ocean from marine plastic litter breakdown, plumbing runoff, production facilities, and other sources. Marine life, including birds, fish, mammals, and plants, ingest microplastics, leading to toxic and mechanical effects such as reduced food intake, suffocation, behavioral changes, and genetic alterations. Notably, people can inhale microplastics from the air, ingest them from water, and even absorb them through the skin. These particles have been found in various human organs, including newborn babies' placentas. Chemicals associated with microplastics can impact human genetics, brain development, and respiration rates, especially in women (Amran et al., 2022). There is need of study this plastic pollution crisis, understanding the health risks posed by microplastics remains crucial for our long-term well-being and marine ecosystems. Remember that microplastics are a developing threat to both human and planetary health and understanding their impact is crucial for sustainable management.

2. Objectives:

- To understand the impact of Microplastics on various organisms, including their mechanisms on toxicity and long-term effects.
- To understand the health risk associated with Microplastics.

3. Methodology:

The Research design adopted in this study was descriptive and the data was collected through structural questions from numerous respondents.

4. The Effect of Microplastics on Soil Ecosystem:

Microplastics, which are tiny plastic particles less than 5 mm in size, have been increasingly recognized as a global environmental concern. While much attention has been focused on their impact in marine environments, their effects on soil ecosystems are also significant and concerning such as:

I.   Physical Effects: Microplastics can alter soil structure and water retention capabilities. Their presence can affect soil porosity and compaction, potentially impacting root growth and nutrient uptake by plants.

II.   Chemical Effects: Microplastics can absorb and accumulate harmful chemical pollutants from the surrounding environment. These pollutants can include pesticides, heavy metals, and organic contaminants. When microplastics are present in soil, they can act as carriers for these pollutants, potentially increasing their bioavailability and toxicity to soil organisms and plants.

III.   Biological Effects: Soil organisms such as earthworms, microorganisms, and small invertebrates can ingest microplastics either directly or indirectly through contaminated soil or organic matter. This ingestion can lead to physical harm (e.g., blockage of digestive tracts), physiological stress, and even transfer of plastics and associated pollutants up the food chain.

IV.   Ecological Impacts: The introduction of microplastics into soil ecosystems can disrupt microbial communities and nutrient cycling processes. Microplastics may also alter the composition and diversity of soil fauna and flora, affecting overall ecosystem health and resilience.

5. Microplastics Impact on Human Health:

The microplastics can enter the human body through ingestion, inhalation, or even through the skin. Once get inside the human body, they may cause harm by accumulating in organs, triggering inflammation, or releasing toxic substances (Mudgal et al., 2010). Recent evidence indicates that humans constantly inhale and ingest microplastics through contaminated seafood, including fish and shellfish. Additionally, microplastics have been found in tap water, bottled water, and even commonly consumed beverages, such as beer and salt. In fact, a new system estimates that the average adult consumes approximately 2,000 microplastics per year through salt. Different chemicals can leach from the plastic water bottles, knives and dermatologic products to enter our bodies. These compounds are linked to serious health issues such as endocrine disruption, weight gain, insulin resistance, decreased reproductive health, and cancer.

6. Toxicology of Microplastics: TOXIMP:

The toxicological effects of microplastics encompass a range of impacts on both aquatic and terrestrial organisms. These tiny plastic particles, often less than 5 mm in size, can cause physical harm when ingested, potentially leading to abrasions or blockages in the gastrointestinal tract of marine animals and other wildlife (Ghosh et al., 2023). Additionally, microplastics act as carriers for toxic pollutants such as heavy metals and organic chemicals, which can adhere to their surfaces. Upon ingestion, these pollutants may leach into the tissues of organisms, causing oxidative stress, inflammation, and disrupting hormonal systems through endocrine disruption (Kumar et al., 2020). This can lead to broader ecological implications, including bioaccumulation in the food chain and bio magnification to higher trophic levels, potentially impacting reproductive success, developmental processes, and overall population health of affected species. While direct human health impacts from ingesting or inhaling microplastics are still under investigation, there is growing concern about the potential for microplastics and associated contaminants to enter the human food chain through seafood consumption and drinking water. Regulatory responses are gradually emerging, with some countries and regions implementing bans or restrictions on microplastics in consumer products, alongside efforts to develop monitoring programs and mitigation strategies to reduce environmental contamination. Continued research is crucial to fully understand the long-term toxicological effects of microplastics and to develop effective strategies for their management and control.

7. POPs (Persistent Organic Pollutants):

The interaction between microplastics and persistent organic pollutants (POPs) in soil ecosystems is a complex environmental issue with several key impacts. Microplastics, due to their small size and durability, can accumulate POPs from various sources such as industrial runoff, agricultural chemicals, and atmospheric deposition (Anik et al., 2021). Once these POPs adhere to Microplastics surfaces, they become more resistant to degradation and can persist in soil for extended periods (Yang et al., 2022). This persistence increases the potential for POPs to be transported within soil profiles through processes like erosion and leaching, potentially contaminating groundwater sources. In soil, microplastics can be ingested by soil-dwelling organisms such as earthworms, insects, and microorganisms. The presence of POPs on microplastics means that these contaminants can bio accumulate in the tissues of these organisms over time. This bioaccumulation can lead to adverse effects on organism health and ecosystem functioning, including disruptions to reproductive cycles, immune responses, and overall biodiversity. Furthermore, microplastics can affect soil structure and nutrient cycling processes. Their presence can alter soil physical properties, such as water retention and aeration, which in turn can impact plant growth and soil fertility. This alteration in soil conditions can have cascading effects on agricultural productivity and ecosystem services provided by soils.

Human health risks arise from the potential for POPs to enter the food chain through contaminated soil (Passuello et al., 20210). Crops grown in soil containing microplastics and POPs may uptake these contaminants, leading to potential exposure for consumers. This exposure route underscores the importance of monitoring soil contamination levels and implementing measures to mitigate Microplastics pollution in agricultural and urban soils. Addressing the issue of microplastics and POPs in soil requires integrated approaches, including improved waste management practices, regulation of chemical use, and development of remediation technologies. Research efforts are crucial to better understand the fate, transport, and ecological impacts of microplastics and associated contaminants in soil ecosystems, ensuring sustainable soil management and protection of environmental and human health in the long term.

8. PCBs (Polychlorinated Biphenyls):

Polychlorinated biphenyls (PCBs) are persistent organic pollutants known for their detrimental effects on environmental and human health. When PCBs adhere to microplastics, these particles can act as vectors, introducing PCB contamination into soil and impacting the broader environment (Qing et al., 2006). In soil ecosystems, microplastics can accumulate PCBs through various pathways, including atmospheric deposition, runoff from contaminated surfaces, and direct disposal of plastic waste. Once deposited in soil, microplastics can persist for extended periods, releasing PCBs into the environment over time due to their slow degradation rate. PCBs on microplastics pose several significant threats to soil health and ecological balance. Soil-dwelling organisms such as earthworms, insects, and microorganisms may ingest microplastics, leading to the bioaccumulation of PCBs in their tissues. This bioaccumulation can disrupt physiological processes, impair reproductive functions, and compromise immune responses in affected organisms. Furthermore, PCB-contaminated microplastics can alter soil microbial communities and nutrient cycling dynamics, potentially reducing soil fertility and affecting plant growth (Kumar et al., 2022). The mobility of microplastics in soil also raises concerns about the transfer of PCBs to groundwater and surface water bodies through leaching and runoff. This contamination pathway can further exacerbate environmental pollution and pose risks to aquatic ecosystems and human water supplies. Human health risks associated with PCB-contaminated microplastics in soil include potential exposure through the consumption of contaminated crops or drinking water sourced from contaminated areas. PCBs are known to accumulate in the food chain, leading to long-term health effects such as developmental disorders, immune system suppression, and increased risk of certain cancers. To mitigate these risks, strategies for managing Microplastics pollution in soil should include improved waste management practices, remediation technologies to remove contaminants from soil, and regulatory measures to limit the use and release of PCBs and microplastics into the environment. Research efforts focusing on the fate, transport, and toxicity of PCBs on microplastics are essential to develop effective mitigation strategies and safeguard both environmental and human health from the impacts of these persistent pollutants.

9. Critical Analysis:

Survey interpretation: With the help of survey we came to know that majority of the people were aware about Microplastics and it's effects. As The survey results are enumerated below:

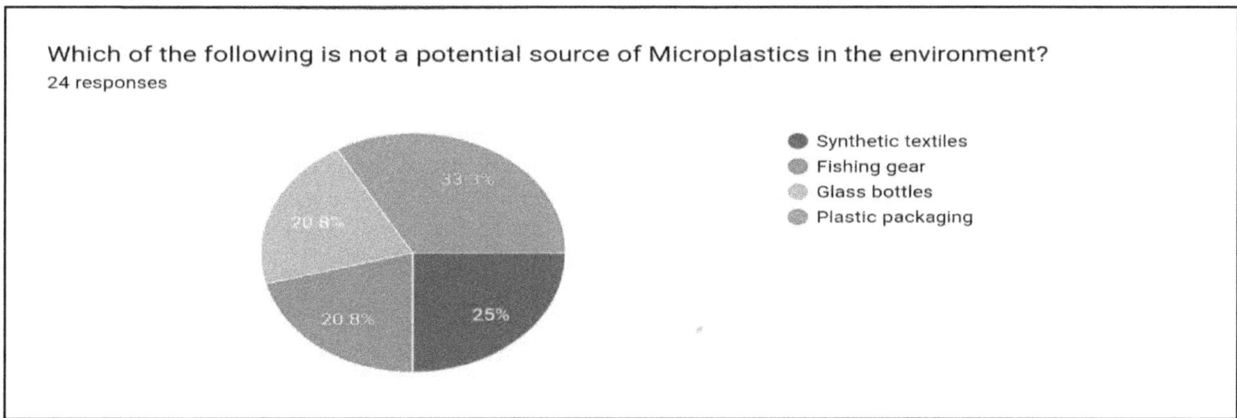

20.8% of the people were given their answers rightly. Glass bottles are not a potential source of microplastics in the environment because they are made entirely of glass, which is a non-plastic material. Microplastics are tiny plastic particles less than 5 millimeters in size that come from the degradation of larger plastic items or are intentionally manufactured at a small scale. Since glass does not degrade into micro-sized particles like plastics do, glass bottles do not contribute to the microplastics pollution in the environment

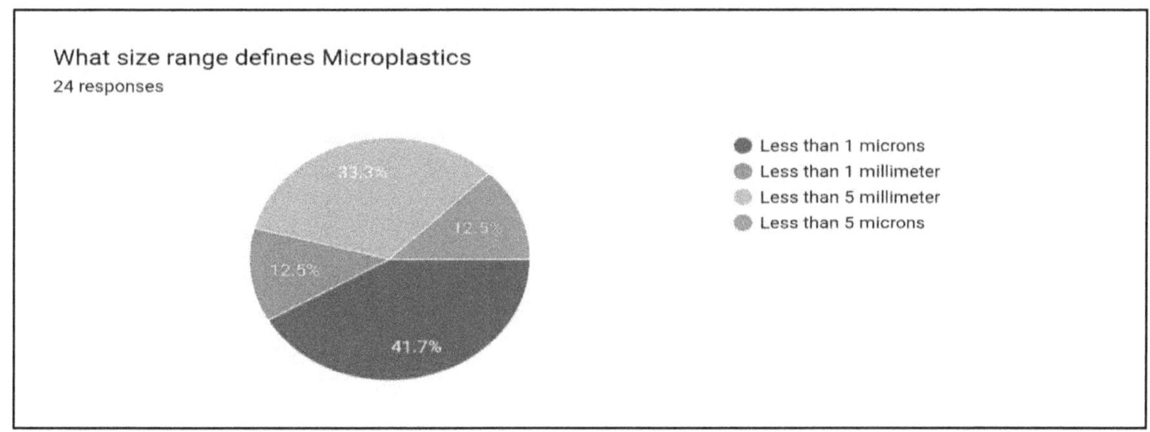

33.3% of the people are correctly given their responses. Microplastics are plastic particles that are smaller than 5 millimeter in size. They result from the breakdown of larger plastic items and pose environmental and health risks when ingested by marine organisms and potentially entering the food chain.

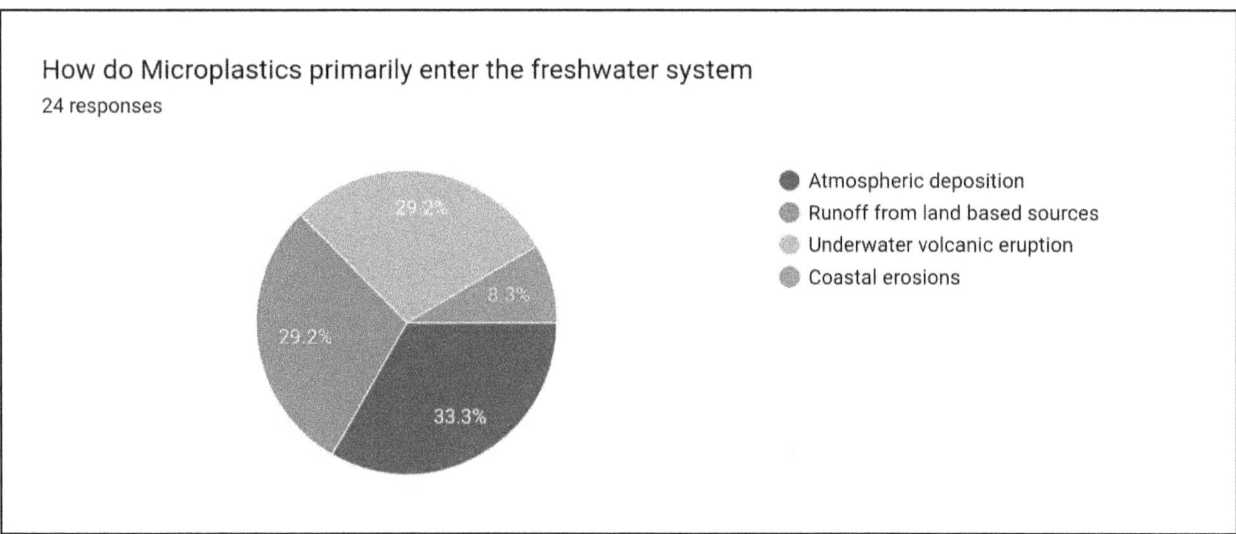

29.2% of the people are given their response correctly. Microplastics primarily enter freshwater systems through runoff from land-based sources, such as urban areas, agricultural runoff, and industrial discharges.

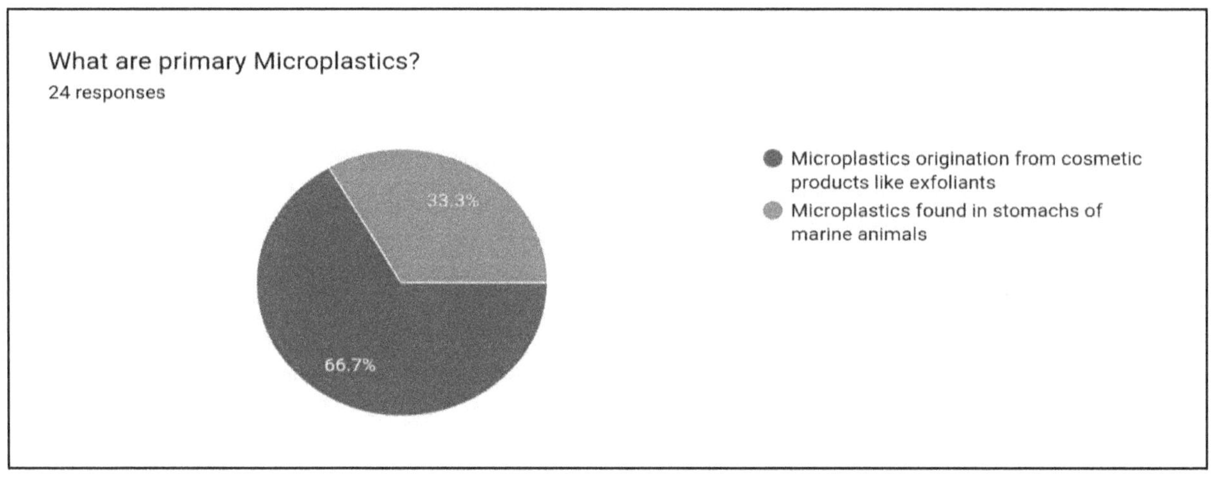

As 66.7% of the people are responded rightly. Microplastics originating from cosmetic products like exfoliants are tiny plastic particles that are intentionally added to these products to enhance their abrasive qualities. However, they are harmful to the environment because they can't be

easily filtered out during wastewater treatment and end up in oceans, where they pose serious threats to marine life and ecosystems.

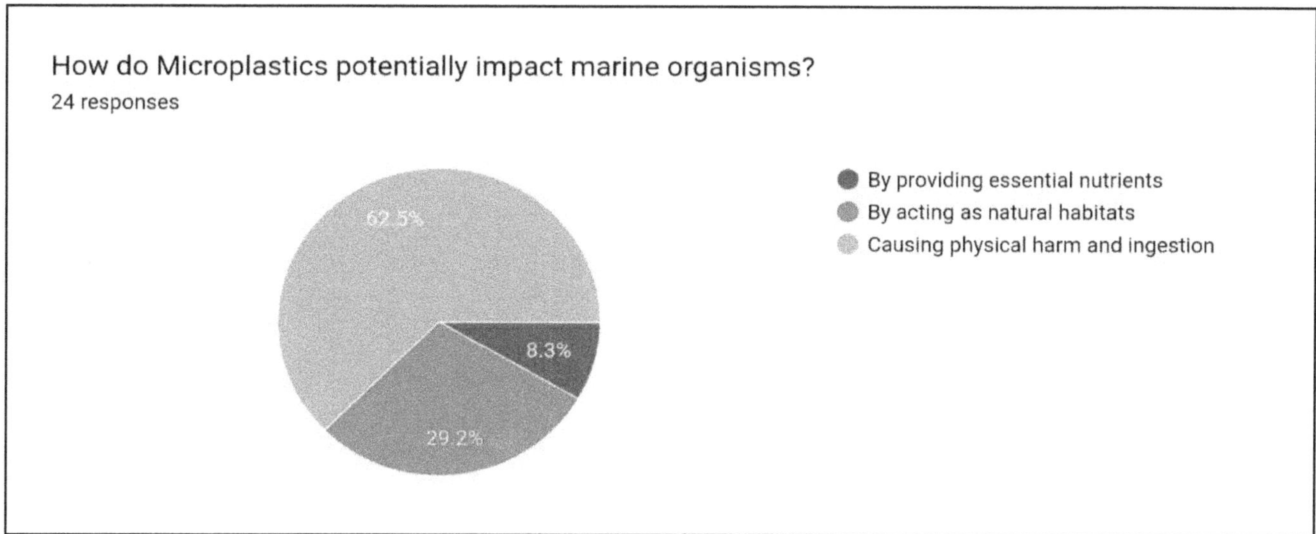

62.5% of the people are responded rightly. The Microplastics potentially impact marine organisms by causing physical harm and ingestion. As they can physically harm microorganisms by causing abrasions and lesions on their surfaces. Additionally, microorganisms can ingest microplastics, leading to blockages, reduced feeding efficiency, and potential toxicity due to chemical additives in the plastics.

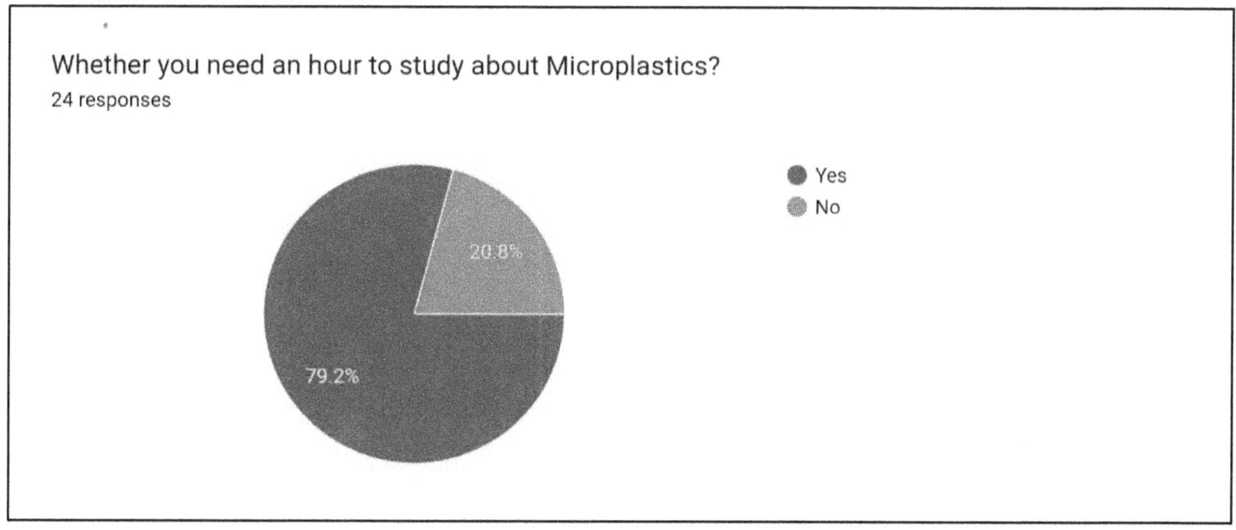

79.2% of the people are responded that they need an hour to study about Microplastics. It is fully depend on the individual person if he/ she want to know more can invest more time to get a full knowledge about it.

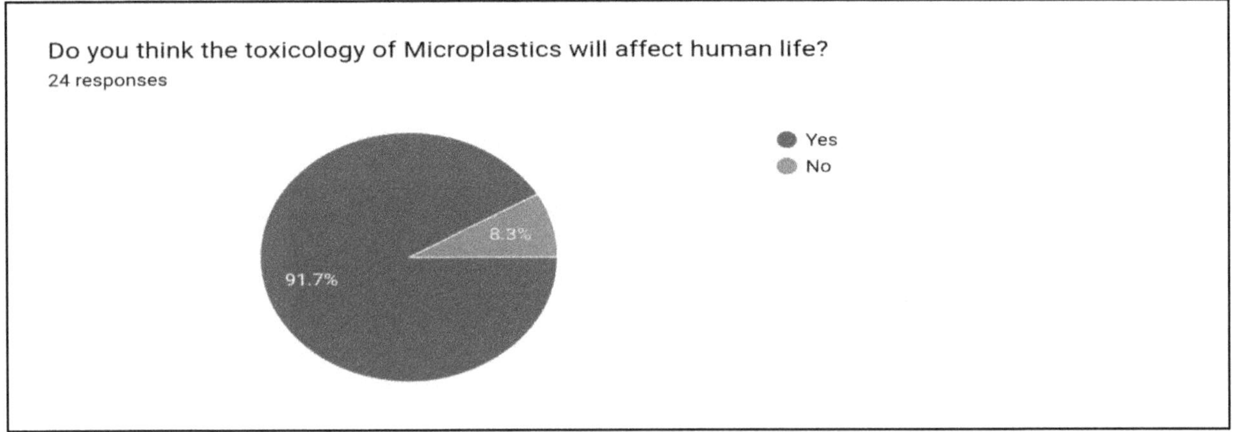

91.7%of the people were responded correctly. The toxicology of microplastics is a concern for human health. These tiny plastic particles can absorb and release harmful chemicals, potentially causing various health effects when ingested or inhaled over time.

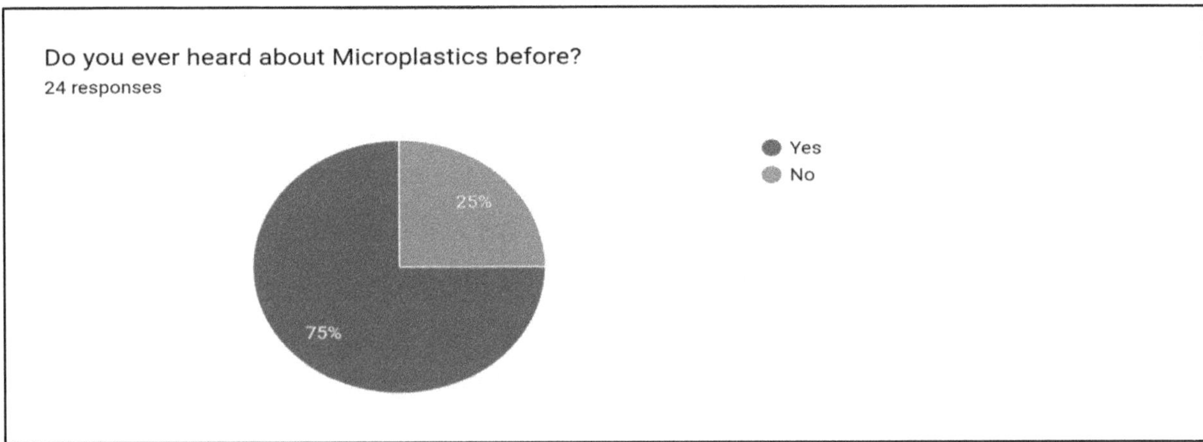

As per the survey we came to know that 75%of the people were already aware of the term Microplastics.

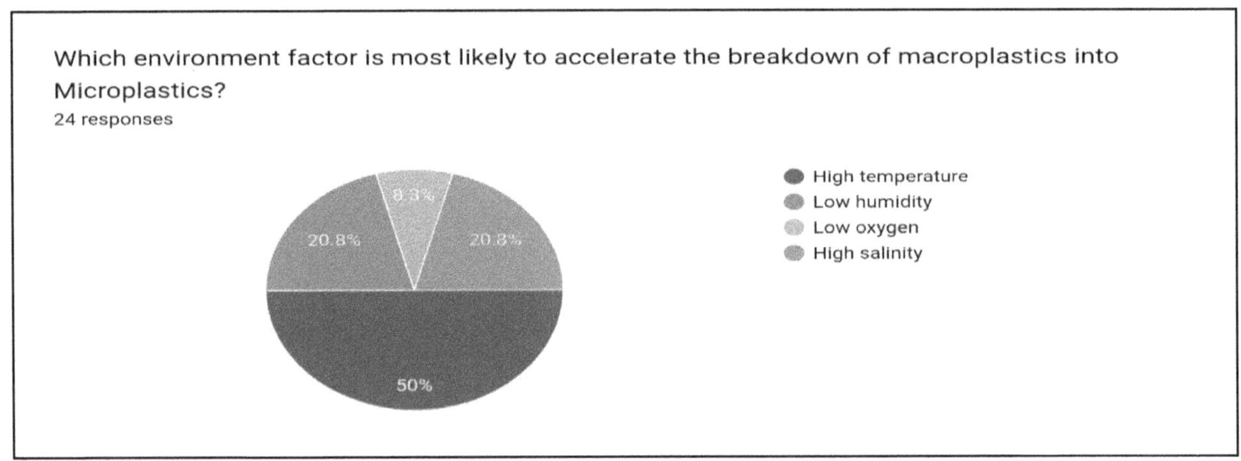

50% of the people were given a response correctly. As High temperatures increase the rate of breakdown of macro plastics into microplastics because they accelerate physical and chemical processes like thermal degradation, increased kinetic energy, and accelerated weathering, all of which fragment larger plastic pieces into smaller ones more rapidly.

10. Suggestions and Recommendation for Future:

Suggestions and recommendation for the future to reduce the impact of microplastics on soil ecosystems, proactive measures and policies must be implemented. First and foremost, reducing plastic consumption at the source is crucial. This involves promoting sustainable alternatives and encouraging industries to innovate towards biodegradable materials. Improved waste management systems are equally vital, ensuring that plastics are properly collected, recycled, or disposed of to prevent them from entering soil environments. Legislative actions should include bans or regulations on the use of microplastics in consumer products like cosmetics and detergents, which are significant sources of microplastics contamination. Public education campaigns are essential to raise awareness about the detrimental effects of microplastics on soil health and ecosystems, fostering behavior changes towards more responsible consumption and disposal practices. These are must be made in the future into order to reduce the detrimental effects of Microplastics soil ecosystem.

11. Conclusion:

This paper can be concluded that microplastics pose a significant environmental challenge globally. Their pervasive presence in marine and terrestrial ecosystems underscores the urgent need for comprehensive research, effective waste management strategies, and stringent regulations to mitigate their detrimental effects. Addressing microplastics pollution requires concerted efforts across sectors to safeguard biodiversity, ecosystem health, and ultimately, human well-being in a sustainable manner.

Reference:

16. Amran, N. H., Zaid, S. S. M., Mokhtar, M. H., Manaf, L. A., & Othman, S. (2022). Exposure to microplastics during early developmental stage: review of current evidence. *Toxics, 10*(10), 597.

17. Anik, A. H., Hossain, S., Alam, M., Sultan, M. B., Hasnine, M. T., & Rahman, M. M. (2021). Microplastics pollution: A comprehensive review on the sources, fates, effects, and

potential remediation. *Environmental Nanotechnology, Monitoring & Management, 16,* 100530.

18. Chen, Y., Chen, Q., Zhang, Q., Zuo, C., & Shi, H. (2022). An overview of chemical additives on (micro) plastic fibers: occurrence, release, and health risks. *Reviews of Environmental Contamination and Toxicology, 260*(1), 22.

19. Ghosh, S., Sinha, J. K., Ghosh, S., Vashisth, K., Han, S., & Bhaskar, R. (2023). Microplastics as an emerging threat to the global environment and human health. *Sustainability, 15*(14), 10821.

20. Kumar, M., Sarma, D. K., Shubham, S., Kumawat, M., Verma, V., Prakash, A., & Tiwari, R. (2020). Environmental endocrine-disrupting chemical exposure: role in non-communicable diseases. *Frontiers in public health, 8,* 553850.

21. Kumar, V., Agrawal, S., Bhat, S. A., Américo-Pinheiro, J. H. P., Shahi, S. K., & Kumar, S. (2022). Environmental impact, health hazards, and plant-microbes synergism in remediation of emerging contaminants. *Cleaner chemical engineering, 2,* 100030.

22. Mudgal, V., Madaan, N., Mudgal, A., Singh, R. B., & Mishra, S. (2010). Effect of toxic metals on human health. *The open Nutraceuticals journal, 3*(1).

23. Passuello, A., Mari, M., Nadal, M., Schuhmacher, M., & Domingo, J. L. (2010). POP accumulation in the food chain: integrated risk model for sewage sludge application in agricultural soils. *Environment international, 36*(6), 577-583.

24. Qing Li, Q., Loganath, A., Seng Chong, Y., Tan, J., & Philip Obbard, J. (2006). Persistent organic pollutants and adverse health effects in humans. *Journal of Toxicology and Environmental Health, Part A, 69*(21), 1987-2005.

25. Xu, C., Zhang, B., Gu, C., Shen, C., Yin, S., Aamir, M., & Li, F. (2020). Are we underestimating the sources of microplastic pollution in terrestrial environment?. *Journal of hazardous materials, 400,* 123228.

26. Yang, H., Dong, H., Huang, Y., Chen, G., & Wang, J. (2022). Interactions of microplastics and main pollutants and environmental behavior in soils. *Science of the Total Environment, 821,* 153511.

13. A Critical Review n Nanotechnology in Medical Diagnostics and Treatment

Ashly Merin George*, Dr. Hemalatha K

MVM College of Pharmacy, Acharya and BM Reddy College of Pharmacy,

Bengaluru, Karnataka, India

Corresponding author e-mail: ashlymerin@gmail.com

Abstract:

In the last decades, nanotechnology products become a significant research focus on worldwide. This nanotechnological product shown their various activities due to its unique properties of nanomaterials used. For most of the medical treatment and diagnosis, nanotechnology is the preferred method due to its rapid and effectiveness. As a result, the demand of nanomaterials is expanding day by day. In medicine, various applications of nanotechnology proved their potential to revolutionize medical diagnosis, immunization, treatment, and even health care products. The conjugation of nanoparticles (NPs)done by many means: chemically (conjugation), physically (encapsulation), or through adsorption. The use of the suitable loading nanosubstance depends on the application purpose. They can be used to deliver various chemicals (drugs, chemotherapeutic agents, or imaging substances), or biological substances (antigens, antibodies, RNA, or DNA) through endocytosis. The present review provides a brief overview about the structure and shape of available NPs, their applications in the medical sciences, an overview of nanomedicine's unique properties, the current development of new drug delivery systems especially in cancer treatment, as sensors, imaging agents and treatment and also on the challenges of nanomedicine in clinical translation. Nanotechnology application in diagnostics includes as diagnostics, imaging agents, for the diagnosis of infectious diseases, for diagnosis of cancer and as a wearable device. Nanotechnology is used for the treatment of cancer, surgery, ophthalmology, brain disorders, wound treatment and surgery. This review also highlighted on outlook, challenges and safety considerations before clinical practice.

Keywords: Nanotechnology, Nanomaterial, Medical, Diagnosis, DNA

1.Introduction:

The term nanotechnology started to use since 1974 as different nanoformulations such as Nanomaterials, Nanomedicine, Nanovaccines, or Nanotheranostics (Troncarelli et al., 2013). The nanomedicine is the application various tools for the treatment of various medical problems. The main need of nano is that while reducing the particle size can convert a product into more reactive, soluble, and efficient manner (Swain et al., 2015). There are many types of Nanoparticles based on the size, shape, and origin. Generally, the nanoparticles exhibit added advantages compared with conventional preparations as diagnostics and therapeutics (Jurj et al., 2017; Ceña and Játiva, 2018): (1) Biocompatible and mostly safer (2) cross the BBB and other physiological barriers and can efficiently kill intracellular and multiple drug-resistant pathogens (Radulescu et al., 2023). The present review focusses on various applications of nanotechnology products in medical diagnostics and treatment.

Tunable Properties of Nanoparticles (Sindhwani and Chan, 2021):
1. Surface properties: Surface area, Surface charge, hydrophobicity, roughness.
2. Physical properties: Size, Shape, Elasticity, Stiffness, Optical.
3. Chemical properties: Material type, Chemical degradation.
4. Biological properties: Biocompatibility, bioavailability.

Nanoparticle Architecture:

a. Nanocrystals: Nanocrystals are advantageous as an oral delivery system for various problems as for drugs having poorly drug solubility (Möschwitzer and Müller, 2006). So, nanocrystals can be used as an alternative to tackle a product with no potential toxicity.

b. Quantum Dots: These are rapidly emerging form as it is popular as a luminescence probes for most of the biological applications due to their small size (approximately 10 nm in diameter), highly stable in presence of light, tunable optical properties, and multiple actions (Jaiswal et al., 2003). These inorganic-organic composite nanomaterials shown extreme efficiency in diagnosis of cancer *in vivo.*

2. Nanotechnology in Medical Diagnostics:

Nanoparticles are emerging as an important technology for *in vitro* diagnostic devices (Weiss et al., 2020). *In vitro* diagnostic tools aimed to detect proteins, DNA or other biomolecular biomarkers which helps to identify if the patient has any particular disease. Application of nanoparticle is the most interesting area still under unhidden research doors going to reveal. In this article, majorly focussed on advancement of nanoparticles as a diagnostic tool. The most common molecules utilized are antibodies, aptamers or peptides. The transduced signal worked in nanoparticles will works in different ways by changing the colour, fluorescence, magnetic or electrical signal. This principal concept utilized while choosing the nanoparticles enables the choice of the transducer signal.

There are two types of *in vitro* diagnostic technology: heterogeneous and homogeneous. In heterogenous assay, the diagnostic product works by binding to the capture molecule. A popular example of a heterogeneous assay is a gold nanoparticle lateral flow immunoassay. In a lateral flow immunoassay, the utilized membrane is dipped into biological fluid (Wang et al., 2020). Here, the capillary force will work as a mode for flow of gold nanoparticle in the membrane, and the biomarker in the fluid attaches to the gold nanoparticles.

In a homogeneous assay, the difference is that diagnostic process happens in a solution. A bead assay is an example of these types of assays. In diagnostic purpose, nanoparticles work by increasing the functionality of the beads. For example, by adding different emitting quantum dots optically coding can be done on the beads. This coding will simultaneously help in the detection of multiple biomarker targets (Kim et al., 2016). More in-depth studies are required to understand fundamentals for nanoparticle engineering principles and thereby able can rationally design optimized nanoparticles with improved selectivity, efficacy, and safety. Currently, most nanoparticles use nontoxic and biodegradable ingredients, thus the toxicities of the carrier molecules as per expectations can make it mild.

2.1. Nanomaterials as Imaging Agents: Recently, nanomaterials use is increasing abruptly as an aid to improve in biomedical detection as well as in imaging due to unique passive, active and physical targeting properties. Due to their small size, nanoparticles show enhanced permeability and retention (EPR) effects in tumors, with relative increases in local tumor concentrations of contrast agent (Oh et al., 2013). Among all features of the nanoparticle, size plays a major role for tumor imaging. Nanoparticle size having direct relation with regards to biodistribution, blood circulation half-life, cellular uptake, tumor penetration and targeting. As the average renal filtration pore is 10 nm, nanoparticles can easily remove by the renal excretion system Scott and Quaggin, 2015). At the same time, nanoparticles with size over than 100 nm can be imaged by macrophages response like its accumulation in organs with the mononuclear phagocyte system (MPS), such as lymph nodes, liver, spleen and lung (Zhou and Dai, 2018). In addition, several reviews concluded that nanoparticle sizes between 10 to 60 nm have shown their activity through increased cellular uptake.

Now a days, various attempts are carrying out on different nanomaterials because of their unique optical, chemical, and physical properties. They can be used as a contrast agent for controlled biodistribution as well as in multi-model imaging techniques such as ultrasound, MRI, PET and SPECT. Because of leakage in capillaries seen in the cancer tissues, the nanoparticles having a tendency to accumulate in the tumor interstitial spaces. This principle helps in the diagnosis of very small lesions which is difficult to detected through other classical imaging techniques and options (Chapman et al., 2013). So many classes of nanoparticles can be utilized as imaging agent, the physical characters of the QD (like high photostability and resistance to photobleaching) made them as the best nanomaterial for imaging purposes. They can be used as fluorescent probes as well as a highly sensitive low-cost biosensor.

Apart an added advantage of QD is that according to the size of the QD used, the degree of the fluorescent emission of the can be controlled. In addition, QD shown advantages over the classical fluorescent dyes, such as   easy to visualize, and can remain longer in the body. Multimodal imaging technique provides advanced benefits such as the combination of paramagnetic QD for fluorescent imaging at the same time with MRI. So, with a short time, clear imaging can be done.

2.2. Nanotechnology in Diagnostics: Nano diagnostics is an emerging field that widely used due to its nanoscale properties thereby can be used to manipulate and analyze single-molecule systems. With their unique physiochemical and optical characteristics, nanomaterials have given accurate and timely diagnosis for various disease conditions. Multipurpose nanosized sensors were designed to detect different pathological parameters, foreign proteins/antigens, and toxic substances.

Recently, bio-barcodes were also developed to particularly target protein disease markers such as the PSA (prostate specific antigen). Such biosensors can be used to diagnose prostatic cancer priorly based on anti-PSA antibodies. The sensitivity of the newly obtained bio-bar code assay is about one million times more efficient than the conventional methods used (Manuja et al., 2012).

2.3. Nanotechnology for the Diagnosis of Infectious Diseases: For around 15 million deaths, worldwide infectious diseases are responsible, among that HIV infections and other respiratory infections were the leading causes. In this context, nanotechnology can be utilized as in various clinical applications such tissue engineering, drug delivery, bioimaging, and diagnostics (Noah and Ndangili, 2019). So, another approach developed to treat infectious disease was developed known as Point-of-care (POC) diagnosis, carried out by giving more priority to individual patient's care. The advantages of POC diagnostic technologies are its disposability, cost-effectiveness, easy to use, and portability. In this approach, even small volumes of bodily fluids, such as blood, saliva, and urine can be analysed. For global health applications, cost and miniature size were the important factors making POC a modern tool (Wang et al., 2021).

Conjugated polymer nanoparticle (CPN) is another nanomaterial widely used for the treatment based on its π-extended CPs. Conjugated polymer nanoparticles show high fluorescence brightness, low cytotoxicity, excellent photostability, reactive oxygen species (ROS) generation ability, and high photothermal conversion efficiency (PCE), making it as a predominant theragnostic tool (Chen et al., 2022).

Klostranec et al., (2007) developed a diagnostic system by making a combination of quantum dots and microfluidics which made it as a powerful tool for analyzing infectious agents in human serum samples in a multiplexed, high-throughput manner. This Lab-on-Chip system has shown its remarkable sensitivity and speed capacity which helps to detect serum biomarkers seen in bloodborne infectious diseases, such as hepatitis B, hepatitis C, and HIV.

Lateral flow immunoassay (LFIA), is another commonly used technique for rapid diagnosis (due to its low cost, ease of use, and accessibility. To improve the effectiveness of LFIA, Wang et al. introduced an amplification-free fluorescence assay using DNA probes and fluorescent nanoparticle-labelled monoclonal antibodies (Wang et al., 2020). This study sown   100% sensitivity and 99.5% specificity in clinical trials in results especially for detecting the SARS-CoV-2 genome.

2.4. Nanomaterials as Wearable Sensors: Wearable sensors recently got wide acceptance due to its non-invasive, rapid, and real-time monitoring ability of glucose levels in human body fluids (Li and Wen, 2021). These sensors worked based on optical and electrochemical methods. In 2001, the GlucoWatch the first electrochemical wearable glucose sensor was developed by Cygnus, but it was not long-lasting, even it is available in high costs and resulted inconvenience for users. To resolve this issue, later nanomaterials integrated wearable glucose-sensing devices was developed Emaminejad *et al.*, (2017) used carbon nanotubes as the immobilization matrix for GOD and H_2O_2 detection material, resulting in a wearable glucose sensor based on users' perspiration. The principle is that glucose was converted into gluconic acid and H_2O_2 by GOD in the presence of oxygen, and the glucose concentration can be found out by detecting H_2O_2 using extrapolation method. On the other hand, using a composite fibre rGO/polyurethane (PU) modified with oxygen-containing functional groups developed a wearable sensor with high glucose sensitivity. Even in this, the sensor had a selectivity in even low detection limit of 500 nmol/L and high mechanical durability.

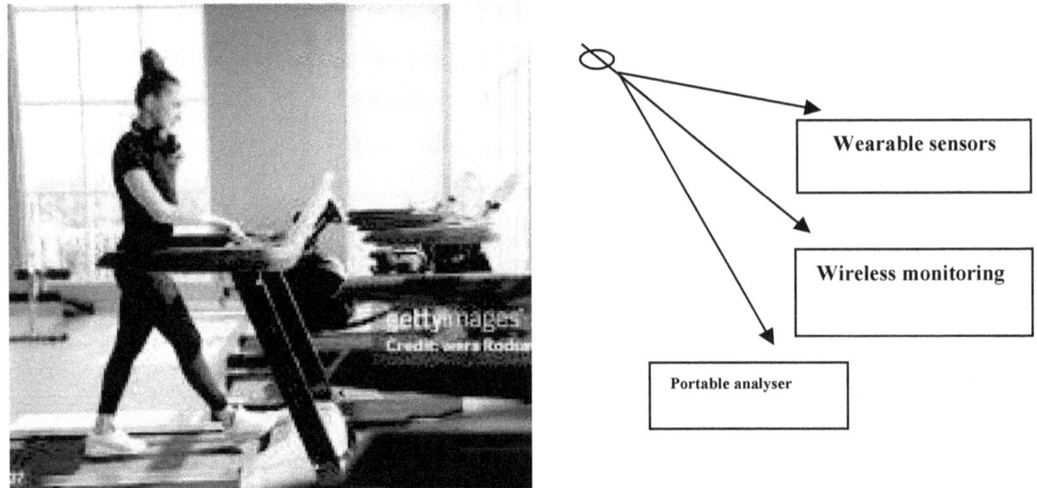

Fig.1 Wireless monitoring

Metal oxide nanomaterials (MONs) are nanomaterials used in the designing of flexible/wearable sensors due to their tunable band gap, low cost and ease of manufacturing. Recently, In_2O_3-nanomaterial-based flexible glucose sensors was reported by using the enzymatic oxidation of d-glucose with glucose oxidase, in which the concentration of d-glucose can be analysed using   pH level determination through enzymatic glucose oxidation. For generalized healthcare applications, the real-time glucose monitoring technology can be utilised as an important approach, Apart from that (Liu et al., 2018), a study result showed that a newly developed wearable In_2O_3 nanoribbon transistor biosensor with chitosan, carbon nanotubes (CNTs), and glucose oxidase coated can be utilised to detect glucose in body fluids.

2.4. Nanotechnology for the Diagnosis of Cancer: The first liposomal nanoparticle product Doxil, which is PEGylated doxorubicin got approval in 1995. It is currently a second-line therapy to chemotherapy for treating ovarian cancer and Kaposi's sarcoma. But those who taken Doxil shown palmar–plantar erythrodysesthesia due to its skin accumulation, thereby leads to reduce the dose of Doxil for patient use (He et al., 2019). Most of the nanoformulations did not improving survival of patient. In this regard, Vyxeous for acute myeloid leukaemia was the first nanomedicine an improved patient survival from 5.9 to 9.6 months during phase III trial.

Chemotherapy is a typical cancer treatment technique that is given to most patients either before or after surgery. But chemotherapeutic drugs resulted in damage to fast-replicating cells especially in the bone marrow, hair follicles, and gastrointestinal system rather than their original target of rapidly dividing malignant cells. The organs and systems affected shown negative consequences and manifestations (Abbas and Rehman, 2018). Thereby chemotherapy doses are limited due to its adverse effects, thereby reduces the treatment's effectiveness. Current therapies have few adverse reactions themselves and, therefore, are inadequate and sometimes needs an alternative to reduce the adverse effects in order to maintain the chemotherapy with required dose (Nurgali et al., 2022). In recent years, in view of this context a significant number of nanomaterials for biomedical applications have been developed and reported. In 2022, Dukle *et al.,* studied on advances on the development of paper-based sensors that can be utilized as an alternative in cancer screening, mostly in low-income countries. For targeting the drugs, drug carriers such as synthetic polymers, microcapsules, liposomes, dendrimers and many others are currently developed and under development process. The increased bio-availability and increased accumulation at the pathological site were the two reasons behind the development of this carrier system. This is especially important for the anticancer drugs, which should preferably be delivered locally with minimal or no effect onto the normal tissue.

Current developments in nanomedicine have demonstrated the enormous potential for drug delivery based on nanotechnology for the diagnosis and treatment of cancer with fewer adverse effects (Tran et al., 2020). Even while nanoparticles are smaller than cells, where NPs' broad surface area gives them a great capacity to bind with ligands, such as small molecules, peptides, and DNA or RNA strands. The nanomaterials used in cancer treatment varies in activity such as blood half-life, biodistribution, interactions and less toxicity due to their varying qualities, based on size, shape, and material characteristics (Kaymaz et al., 2023). NPs are the preferred technique used for diagnosis and treatment of cancer. An overview of the many NP kinds is shown in Fig. 2, which is arranged according to their size range and applications. With the rapid development of nanotechnology, this paper look into various application of nanomaterials especially in cancer diagnosis and treatment with focus on their benefits and limitations during use (Figure 1).

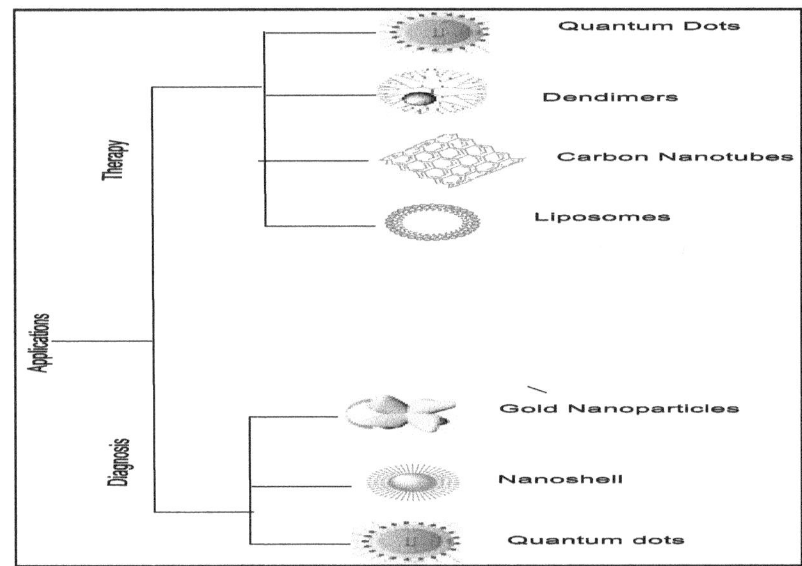

Figure 2: Applications of nanocarriers in both diagnosis and therapy

3. Uses of Nanotechnology in Treatment:

3.1. Nanotechnology for the Treatment of Cancer: In clinical situations, various nanomaterials have significant results. In order to deliver anticancer drugs safely and efficiently to the targeted site in the cancer tissues, anticancer drugs are typically conjugated with nanomaterials. For example, CRLX101 is a novel nanoparticle–drug conjugate of camptothecin that was used in phase Ib/II clinical trials for patients with advanced rectal cancer. The results showed that CRLX101 was well tolerated with only one grade 4 toxicity (lymphopenia), and a pathologic complete response was seen in 19% of patients in the overall cohort and 33% of patients at the maximum tolerated dose (Ekinci et al., 2022). In another clinical trial also the efficacy of the nanoparticle–drug conjugate CRLX101 in combination with bevacizumab was reported in metastatic renal cell carcinoma patients in a phase I-IIa clinical trial.In addition, a first-in-human phase 1/2a trial of CRLX101, a cyclodextrin-containing polymer–camptothecin nanopharmaceutical, was conducted for patients with advanced solid tumor malignancies (Ansari et al., 2020).

Table 1: History of development of smart nanoparticles for cancer diagnosis and treatment

Year	1995	1996	2001	2005	2009	2012	2017
Smart nanproduct	Doxil	DAunoXome	Definity	Abraxane	Ferahamr	Marqibo	Vyxeous

Table 1 depicts the history of development of smart nanoparticles for cancer diagnosis and treatment. Apart some recent developed advanced smart nanoparticles such as black phosphorus (BP), metal-organic framework (MOF), topologically heterogeneous nanoparticles and so on that have attracted more attention due to their unique properties and great potential for cancer therapy. It is widely known that BP has outstanding photothermal properties when exposed to NIR radiation, which made its prevalent smart nanoparticles for cancer photoacoustic (PA) imaging and PTT (Ansari et al., 2020). According to a recent study, an endogenous copper metal-organic framework nanoenzyme has reported which mediate through the synergistic interaction between H_2S-activated NIR PTT for the successful treatment of colon cancer. By avoiding the introduction of cargo, this endogenous biomarker-triggered "turn-on" technique to produce therapeutic molecules *in situ* can be used for simple development of designing nanomedicine especially for the targeted treatment of colon cancer (Deng et al., 2018).

3.2. Nanomaterials for the Treatment of Brain Disorders and Diseases: The brain diseases and disorders" includes a broad range of illnesses that impact the brain, such as infections, tumours, traumas, and neurological abnormalities (Karch, 2017). Among that, brain disorders include illnesses including multiple sclerosis (MS), autism spectrum disorder (ASD), and Alzheimer disease (AD), whereas brain diseases include infections caused by viruses, bacteria, fungi, or parasites. Deterioration of cognitive, motor, and behavioral skills resulting from the impairment of neurological activity is one of the most prominent characteristics of brain diseases and disorders (Baccarini et al., 2020). In medicines, NPs are used in the diagnosis and treatments of different diseases especially brain tumor, metastatic cancers, and neurodegenerative disorders

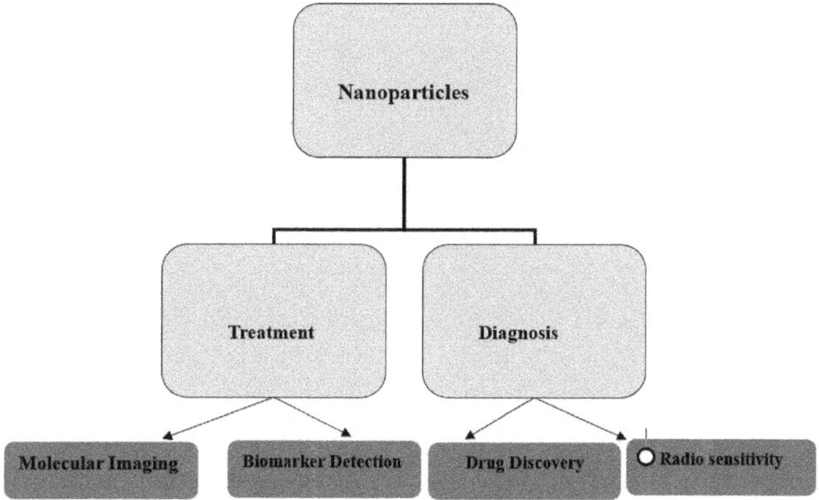

Figure 3: Application of NP's in brain therapy

Treating brain diseases and illnesses has been complicated because of blood-cerebrospinal fluid (CSF) and blood-brain barrier crossings. P-gp plays a significant role in mediating the efflux of materials over the blood-brain barrier, hence its downregulation is linked to the development of tumors and neurodegenerative diseases (Hansson et al., 2009). According to Jablonski et al., 2014) P-gp inhibition increases ability of drug to cross the blood-brain barrier and produce its desired effects. A recent study demonstrated that andrographolide, a neuroprotective medication, has greater BBB permeability when encapsulated in SL NPs as opposed to when the drug is loose. Until now, the three naturally existing allotropes of carbon (amorphous carbon, graphite, and diamond) have been accompanied by allotropes derived from synthetic methods (including carbon nanotubes (CNTs), graphene (GR), nanodiamonds, and fullerenes) (Chae and Lee, 2014). The nanofibre network self-assembly is a radically new strategy for the manufacture of nanostructured materials that encourages and promotes neural regeneration. Various studies showed that by controlling p-gp, NPs can improve the penetration of possible medications and boost their target ability (Silva et al., 2004).

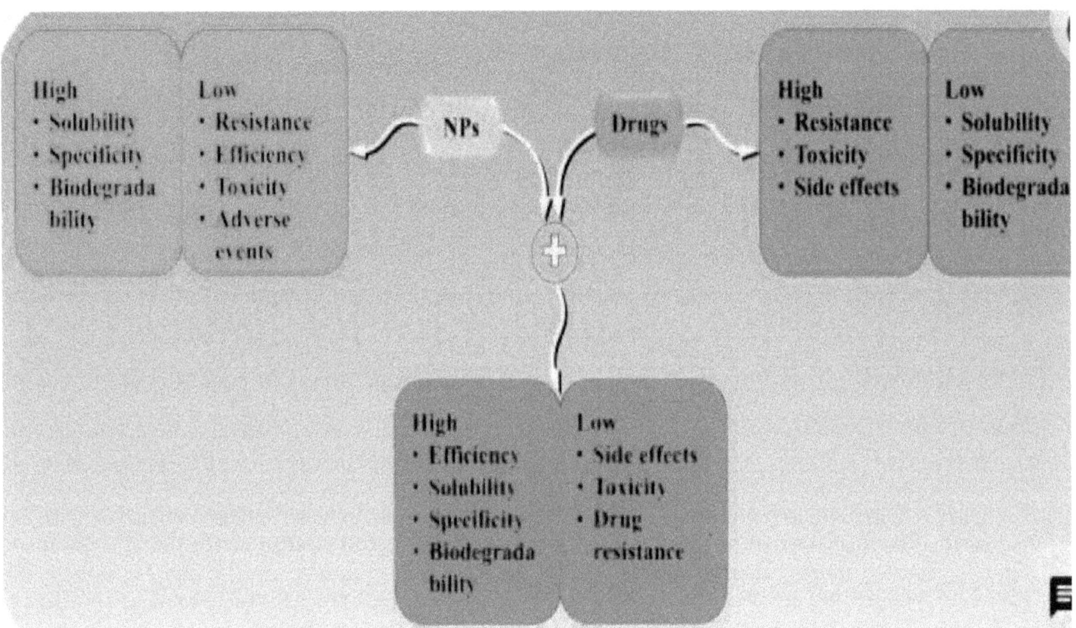

Figure 4: The benefit of drug loading into nanoparticles as opposed to single treatments. Potential medication encapsulation has benefits for NPs and drug properties that offer great efficacy and efficiency

For CNs conditions, early preclinical success for the management of CNS conditions such as, Alzheimer's disease, brain tumors, HIV encephalopathy and acute ischemic stroke has become possible. Alzheimer's disease: Worldwide, more than 35 million people are affected by

Alzheimer's disease (AD), which is the most common form dementia. Nano technology finds significant applications in neurology (Sivaramakrishnan and Neelakantan, 2014). Future development of CNS nanomedicines needs to focus on increasing their drug better performance and specificity for brain tissue using novel targeting moieties

3.3. Applications in Ophthalmology: The current therapeutic challenges in drug delivery, postoperative scarring will be revolutionized with the help of nanotechnology like sight-restoring therapy for patients with retinal degenerative disease (Lanza et al., 1998). Treatments for ophthalmic diseases are expected from this emerging field. A novel nanoscale-dispersed eye ointment (NDEO) for the treatment of severe evaporative dry eye has been successfully developed (Zhang et al., 2014).

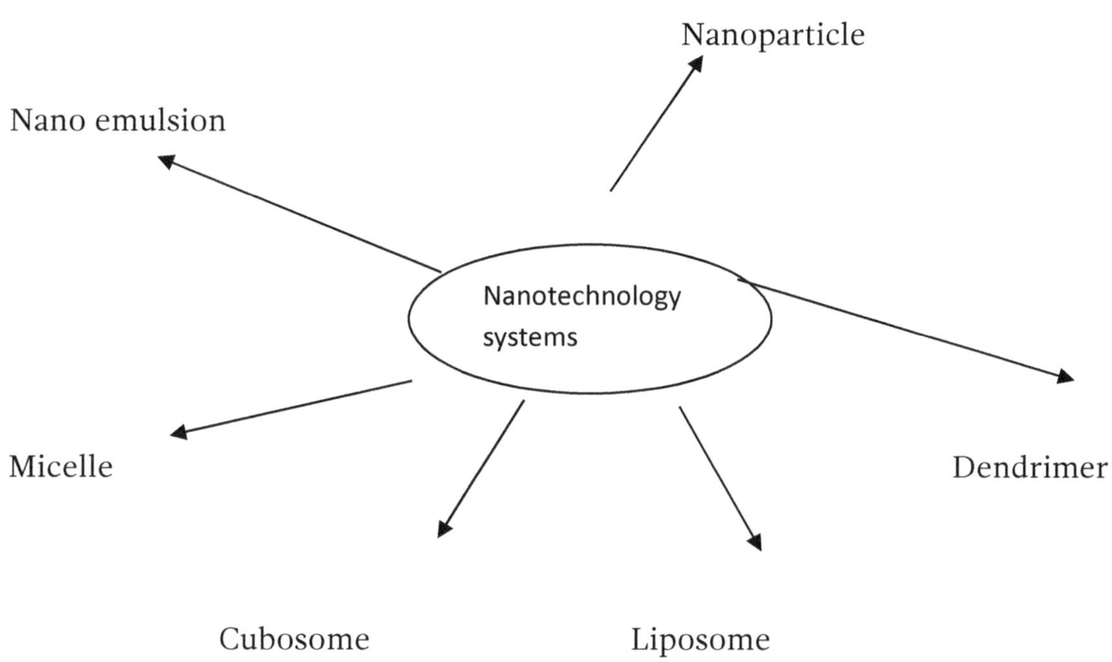

Fig.5: Different nanotechnology systems

Fig .5 shows significant nanotechnology systems recently having immense applications in ophthalmology Among that, micelles are colloidal drug delivery systems that form spontaneously in a solution when the concentration of the polymer/surfactant is above the critical micellar concentration (CMC). Micelles works by enhancing the corneal permeability of topically applied drugs and are good candidates for drug targeting ocular tissues (Vadlapudi et al., 2015).

Durasite technology, a topical polymer-based sustained delivery technology that aids by solubilising drugs in aqueous solutions, utilized in the development of Bromsite®. Eysuvis® approved in 2020, was also developed based on mucus penetrating particle (MPP) technology. This platform helps in optimal penetration of drugs through the mucin layer of the tear film, thereby avoiding loss of drug by nasolacrimal drainage.

3.4. Nanotechnology in Wound Treatment: Due to sickness and damage, if a person's cells lost it can recreate tissues and organs only by reconstructive and transplant. Research into this subject, pointed into the development of nanogenerators, polymer nanoparticles as an alternative solution for wound treatment. Nanoparticles can only be connected with pictures and target ligands to cells or tissue (Popov, 2020). This allows surgeons and radiographers to identify among sick tissue from healthy ones more effectively, improve illness treatment and reduce the danger of harming healthy tissue. Nanotechnology improved the speedy recovery of patient from trauma and specificity of biomarker assessments in bodily fluids. The Applications of nanotechnology for diagnosis, which includes usage of carbon nanotubes, application of gold nanorobs, which is a comparatively quick & inexpensive detections, made illness identification at an earlier stage This technique uses instruments at sub micrometer sizes to diagnose, prevent, and cure illnesses better and improve patients' quality of life. The development of regenerative drugs can be done more effectively using nanotechnology. New approaches allow prosthetic skin, bone, cartilage, or other tissues in patients with organ insufficiency or serious injuries. The use of nanotechnology changes cellular function more effectively to show the same effects of natural tissues and organs. The rapid development of nanomaterials for wound healing has prompted the clinical exploration of nanotherapy-based wound-healing treatments (Haleem. Et al., 2023)

3.5. Nanotechnology for Surgery: A technology developed by Rice University using two pieces of chicken meat fused by a flesh welder, by placing two pieces of chicken touching each other (Stoica et al., 2020). In this technique, green liquid containing gold-coated nano shells is allowed to dribble along the seam and two sides are weld together. This method can be used arteries which have been cut during organ transplant. The flesh welder can be used to weld the artery perfectly. This is an example of studies going in surgery. Numerous novel tools are made available for orthopedic applications using nanotechnology with some coating materials. The most popular coating materials are metalloceramic, hydroxyapatite, and nanostructured diamond (Sahoo et al., 2020).

Recently, robots have been used to do routine surgical procedures, and with the aid of nanobiotechnology, another aspect of robotics has been established (Amirtharaj et al., 2022). This is also referred to as nanobots or nanorobots. These tiny robots are so small that they may be inserted into the body through the vascular system or by catheters. The likelihood of tissue injury while using a traditional LASER is significant, since it produces heat before cutting. By performing an exceedingly accurate surgery, ultra-short pulse lasers are utilized to sever nanosized cell structures, such as nerve cells. " Nano scissors" create low-energy, femtosecond near-infrared laser pulses without endangering the healthy tissues around them. The thermal damage caused by the brief and low-energy laser pulses is modest. Reduced mechanical effects such as plasma extension and shock waves are to blame for this. In addition, there is no buildup of heat and no thermal harm to healthy surrounding tissues. Within 24 h, 50% of the severed axons showed signs of regeneration (Giri et al., 2021). In dermatology, ophthalmology, and corneal refractive surgery, femtosecond laser systems are used

A novel method for preventing surgical infections utilises silver nano-coating on sutures. To control bleeding and mend injured tissues, an aqueous nanoparticle solutions containing Stöber (Mesoporous) silica or iron oxide are employed for nano bridging (Yanik et al., 2004).

3.6. Gene and Stem Cell Therapy: Nanoparticle delivery mechanisms have many benefits,so it is utilized as a carrier by making surface modification with targeting moieties. This technique will help to distribute the drug to the desired cells thereby can minimize susceptible toxicities or unexpected effects.

Nucleus-targeted drug delivery (NTDD) for reversing CSC's drug resistance is another successful approach used in stem cell therapy. Apart in a recent study,a silica nanoparticles based system was developed to attack the nucleus of CSC directly. By surface modulation of anti-CD133 and thermal sensitive exposure of TAT peptides in the presence of opposing magnetic fields, they reached the nucleus (Ali et al., 2023). Results shown that successful nucleus-targeted drug release eventually contributes to CSC apoptosis caused by combination chemotherapy and thermotherapy with hypoxia-activated.

3.7. Nanotechnology for Genetic Editing and Vaccine: Delivery of nucleic acids for genetic editing and vaccines is an emerging area of nanomedicine. Onpattro (patisiran), developed by Alnylam Pharmaceuticals and approved in 2018, is the first successfully translated nanomedicine to deliver nucleic acids. It is a lipid nanoparticle (LNP) platform developed with an outer shell consisting of pH-sensitive cationic lipids and an aqueous core encapsulating negatively charged nucleic acids. It is shielded on the outside by PEG for stability and charge neutrality. Their overall size is less than 100 nm which have a short-interfering RNA (siRNA) for the treatment of hereditary transthyretin amyloidosis (hATTR) (Li et al., 2019). Onpattro delivers the siRNA primarily to liver hepatocytes to silence the TTR gene. The lipid nanoparticles' design adsorbs ApoE during circulation, enabling them to bind to the hepatocytes' LDL or VLDL receptors (Adams et al., 2018).

3.8. Nanotechnology in Operative Dentistry: A wide variety of materials are using for the treatment of tooth decay by the incorporation of materials such as nanocomposites, nano bonding systems, nano varnish and sealants (Akinc et al., 2019).

4. Approved Nanodrugs and Ongoing Trials on Nanotechnological Products:
The success of nanomaterials in clinical trials is reflected by more than 250 US Food and Drug Administration–approved nanodrugs available on the market. Some of the interesting drugs include Doxil (doxorubicin HCL liposome injection), Invega Sustenna (paliperidone palmitate), DepoCyt (liposomal cytarabine), and Plegridy (PEGylated interferon β-1a) used for the treatment of multiple myeloma, schizophrenia, lymphomatous meningitis, and MS (Reddy et al., 2020), respectively.

Moreover, according to study results by Abdolahi et al., 2017 shown that treatment with omega-3 fatty acids and curcumin NPs significantly reduces inflammation in migraine patients by suppressing the expressions of TNF-α, intercellular adhesive molecule 1, and cooxygenase-2/inducible nitric oxide synthase.

5. Importance of Safety Considerations for Smart Nanoparticles Towards Clinical Use:

I. Preclinical evaluation: Prior to clinical trials, extensive preclinical evaluations are necessary to investigate the safety profile of smart nanoparticles.
II. Systemic toxicity: Smart nanoparticles should undergo rigorous evaluation to determine their systemic toxicity. This includes examining their distribution in the body, potential accumulation in organs.
III. Immunotoxicity assessment: Immunotoxicity studies are essential to evaluate any immune reactions, including inflammation or immunosuppression, caused by the nanoparticles. Understanding the immune implications helps to determine the

compatibility of nanoparticles with the immune system and their potential for immunomodulatory applications.

IV. Targeted toxicity: This involves investigating if the nanoparticles induce any cytotoxicity or unwanted effects in the vicinity of the target area.

V. Pharmacokinetics and biodistribution: This information helps to assess potential accumulation in critical organs, elimination pathways, and the overall clearance of the nanoparticles, minimizing the risk of toxicity and ensuring safe clinical use.

VI. Long-term safety: These evaluations involve prolonged exposure studies to monitor any chronic toxicity, including the nanoparticles' potential to induce tumorigenic effects or chronic inflammation.

VII. Regulatory compliance: Regulatory authorities, such as the FDA, require comprehensive safety data to support the approval of nanoparticle-based therapies. By addressing these safety considerations, researchers and clinicians can establish a solid foundation of evidence regarding the safety and toxicity of smart nanoparticles.

6. Challenges and Outlook:

Recently nanomedicine have made a remarkable space in diagnostics as well as in treatment. Recent success includes Vyxeous and COVID-19 vaccines from Pfizer-BioNTech and Moderna. However, many other companies failed clinical trials or are still searching for the optimal design for their clinical applications (Ventola, 2017). These failures have paved a way to find out why formulations, trials and companies failed. This has intensified research effort in the last decade towards understanding the basics regarding nanoparticle– biological (nano-bio) interactions. Understanding challenges, failures and successes of nanoparticles for clinical applications is key to future nanomedicine success (He et al., 2019). The nano-bio interaction studies have identified key nanoparticle–biological barriers to delivery, which may guide the selection of disease targets.

The cost/benefit analysis of the emerging trends and future outlooks discussed in this article indicates several advantages and challenges. One of the benefits of the emerging trends in POC diagnostics is the potential for more efficient and intelligent diagnosis, which can lead to quicker results. This can result in improved patient outcomes and reduced healthcare costs. Additionally, the combination of novel biosensors, nanotechnology, and AI techniques can automate diagnostic processes, reduce human error, and increase the accuracy and speed of diagnosis. AI algorithms, such as machine learning and deep learning, can be applied to medical data analysis to generate insights that can improve patient outcomes and reduce healthcare costs (Sun et al., 2020). AI can aid in medical diagnosis, drug development, and patient care, and can revolutionize the way medical data are analyzed, leading to speedy and more accurate diagnosis.

Biosensors commonly employ nanomaterials with intricate structures to enhance detection. However, these nanomaterials often exhibit varying morphologies between batches, leading to poor reproducibility. Therefore, further research is necessary to gain a better understanding of the nanomanufacturing process, how to control particle aggregation, and regulate surface interactions. Strict quality control measures are also essential for clinical applications to make it as a reliable method of measurement. Another challenge is inability to detect multiple molecules at once, as current assays are often limited to a single analyte. However, studying multiple substances simultaneously can provide more comprehensive information and enhance detection efficiency, especially in cases where sample volume is less.

Nanomaterials in wound healing have potential benefits, but regulatory considerations having challenges. Extensive testing is needed to ensure safety and efficacy, and clear guidelines and standards are needed for manufacturing, labelling, and use Regulatory bodies must also have to address about the potential toxicity and environmental impact of these nanoparticles (Souza et al., 2019). Lastly, in developing countries, the problem of accessibility to healthcare is a big deal, due to financial limitations, a shortage of skilled personnel, and a lack of infrastructure. The lack of includes access to running water, refrigeration, and electricity. Strategies should include a strategy for the development of an inexpensive POC testing devices operated with solar-rechargeable batteries instead of electricity; the creation of more devices manufactured with abundant, locally available raw material, e.g., paper-based LFAs; and the introduction of POC testing devices with assays that require minimal or no sample preparation and the use of smartphone cameras as spectrographs instead of expensive spectrometers for obtaining results. All these new areas have to be addressed for improvement of the healthcare system and improving the survival rate in developing countries.

7. Conclusion:

This review discussed on recent advancements in diagnostics and in treatment. With nanotechnology, diagnostics shown performance at the nanoscale, resulting in the use of handy devices that are easy to operate and affordable. Nanoparticle-based platforms have been developed for the treatment of infectious disease, as biomarkers, making diagnostic procedures less with increased sensitivity. Multiplexing can be attained through the integration of nanomaterials and artificial intelligence. Various nanomaterials based on the physical and chemical properties of their surface have been used as a drug delivery system, optical imaging, surgery, stem cell therapy. In addition, nanotechnology utilized in gene therapy and vaccine preparation. NPs have many merits in immunization and vaccine production due to its fewer side effects following vaccination and controlled release of the antigens, target directly to the tissues, and need smaller volumes. NPs can also act by activating active immune response by carrying multiple antigens without degradation. The nature of these immune responses is affected by size of NPs, the materials used in manufacturing NPs, type of coating, and surface charge. However, the strategy for the need for the development of cost-effective devices, its significance and challenges discussed. After further exploration, the potential of nanotechnology in treatment of various diseases and as diagnostics will be limitless.

References:

1. Troncarelli, M. Z., Brandão, H. M., Gern, J. C., Guimarães, A. S., & Langoni, H. (2013). Nanotechnology and antimicrobials in veterinary medicine. *Formatex, 13*, 543-556.

2. Swain, P. S., Rajendran, D., Rao, S. B. N., & Dominic, G. (2015). Preparation and effects of nano mineral particle feeding in livestock: A review. *Veterinary world, 8*(7), 888.

3. Jurj, A., Braicu, C., Pop, L. A., Tomuleasa, C., Gherman, C. D., & Berindan-Neagoe, I. (2017). The new era of nanotechnology, an alternative to change cancer treatment. *Drug design, development and therapy*, 2871-2890.

4. Ceña, V., & Játiva, P. (2018). Nanoparticle crossing of blood–brain barrier: a road to new therapeutic approaches to central nervous system diseases. Nanomedicine, 13(13), 1513-1516.

5. Radulescu, D. M., Surdu, V. A., Ficai, A., Ficai, D., Grumezescu, A. M., & Andronescu, E. (2023). Green synthesis of metal and metal oxide nanoparticles: a review of the principles and biomedical applications. *International Journal of Molecular Sciences, 24*(20), 15397.

6. Sindhwani, S., & Chan, W. C. (2021). Nanotechnology for modern medicine: next step towards clinical translation. *Journal of Internal Medicine, 290*(3), 486-498.

7. Möschwitzer, J., & Müller, R. H. (2006). New method for the effective production of ultrafine drug nanocrystals. *Journal of nanoscience and nanotechnology, 6*(9-10), 3145-3153.

8. Jaiswal, J. K., Mattoussi, H., Mauro, J. M., & Simon, S. M. (2003). Long-term multiple color imaging of live cells using quantum dot bioconjugates. *Nature biotechnology, 21*(1), 47-51.

9. Weiss, C., Carriere, M., Fusco, L., Capua, I., Regla-Nava, J. A., Pasquali, M., ... & Delogu, L. G. (2020). Toward nanotechnology-enabled approaches against the COVID-19 pandemic. *ACS nano, 14*(6), 6383-6406.

10. Wang, X., Xiong, E., Tian, T., Cheng, M., Lin, W., Wang, H., ... & Zhou, X. (2020). Clustered regularly interspaced short palindromic repeats/Cas9-mediated lateral flow nucleic acid assay. *ACS nano, 14*(2), 2497-2508.

11. Kim, J., Biondi, M. J., Feld, J. J., & Chan, W. C. (2016). Clinical validation of quantum dot barcode diagnostic technology. *ACS nano, 10*(4), 4742-4753.

12. Oh, I. H., Min, H. S., Li, L., Tran, T. H., Lee, Y. K., Kwon, I. C., ... & Huh, K. M. (2013). Cancer cell-specific photoactivity of pheophorbide a–glycol chitosan nanoparticles for photodynamic therapy in tumor-bearing mice. *Biomaterials, 34*(27), 6454-6463.

13. Scott, R. P., & Quaggin, S. E. (2015). Beyond the cell: the cell biology of renal filtration. *The Journal of Cell Biology, 209*(2), 199.

14. Zhou, Y., & Dai, Z. (2018). New strategies in the design of nanomedicines to oppose uptake by the mononuclear phagocyte system and enhance cancer therapeutic efficacy. *Chemistry–An Asian Journal, 13*(22), 3333-3340.

15. Chapman, S., Dobrovolskaia, M., Farahani, K., Goodwin, A., Joshi, A., Lee, H., ... & Yang, L. (2013). Nanoparticles for cancer imaging: The good, the bad, and the promise. *Nano today, 8*(5), 454-460.

16. Meena, N., Sahni, Y., Thakur, D., & Singh, R. (2018). Applications of nanotechnology in veterinary. *Vet World, 3*(10), 477-480.

17. Manuja, A., Kumar, B., & Singh, R. K. (2012). Nanotechnology developments: opportunities for animal health and production. *Nanotechnology* Development, 2(1), e4-e4.

18. Nanotechnology for infectious diseases. Nat. Nanotechnol. 2021;16:1. doi: 10.1038/s41565-021-00909-0.

19. Noah, N. M., & Ndangili, P. M. (2019). Current trends of nanobiosensors for point-of-care diagnostics. *Journal of Analytical Methods in Chemistry, 2019*(1), 2179718.

20. Wang, C., Liu, M., Wang, Z., Li, S., Deng, Y., & He, N. (2021). Point-of-care diagnostics for infectious diseases: From methods to devices. *Nano Today, 37*, 101092.

21. Chen, X., Hussain, S., Abbas, A., Hao, Y., Malik, A. H., Tian, X., ... & Gao, R. (2022). Conjugated polymer nanoparticles and their nanohybrids as smart photoluminescent and photoresponsive material for biosensing, imaging, and theranostics. *Microchimica Acta, 189*(3), 83.

22. Klostranec, J. M., Xiang, Q., Farcas, G. A., Lee, J. A., Rhee, A., Lafferty, E. I., ... & Chan, W. C. (2007). Convergence of quantum dot barcodes with microfluidics and signal processing for multiplexed high-throughput infectious disease diagnostics. *Nano letters, 7*(9), 2812-2818.

23. Wang, D., He, S., Wang, X., Yan, Y., Liu, J., Wu, S., ... & Tang, Y. (2020). Rapid lateral flow immunoassay for the fluorescence detection of SARS-CoV-2 RNA. *Nature Biomedical Engineering, 4*(12), 1150-1158.

24. Li, G., & Wen, D. (2021). Sensing nanomaterials of wearable glucose sensors. *Chinese Chemical Letters, 32*(1), 221-228.

25. Emaminejad, S., Gao, W., Wu, E., Davies, Z. A., Yin Yin Nyein, H., Challa, S., ... & Davis, R. W. (2017). Autonomous sweat extraction and analysis applied to cystic fibrosis and glucose monitoring using a fully integrated wearable platform. *Proceedings of the National Academy of sciences, 114*(18), 4625-4630.

26. Liu Q., Liu Y., Wu F., Cao X., Li Z., Alharbi M., Abbas A.N., Amer M.R., Zhou C. (2018).Highly Sensitive and Wearable In_2O_3 Nanoribbon Transistor Biosensors with Integrated On-Chip Gate for Glucose Monitoring in Body Fluids. *ACS Nano.*12:1170–1178. doi: 10.1021/acsnano.7b06823.

27. He, H., Liu, L., Morin, E. E., Liu, M., & Schwendeman, A. (2019). Survey of clinical translation of cancer nanomedicines—lessons learned from successes and failures. *Accounts of chemical research, 52*(9), 2445-2461.

28. Abbas, Z., & Rehman, S. (2018). An overview of cancer treatment modalities. *Neoplasm, 1*, 139-157.

29. Nurgali, K., Rudd, J. A., Was, H., & Abalo, R. (2022). Cancer therapy: The challenge of handling a double-edged sword. *Frontiers in Pharmacology, 13*, 1007762.

30. Dukle A., Nathanael A.J., Panchapakesan B., Oh T.-H (2022). Role of Paper-Based Sensors in Fight against Cancer for the Developing World. *Biosensors*;12:737. doi: 10.3390/bios12090737

31. Tran, P., Lee, S. E., Kim, D. H., Pyo, Y. C., & Park, J. S. (2020). Recent advances of nanotechnology for the delivery of anticancer drugs for breast cancer treatment. *Journal of Pharmaceutical Investigation, 50*, 261-270.

32. Kaymaz, S. V., Nobar, H. M., Sarıgül, H., Soylukan, C., Akyüz, L., & Yüce, M. (2023). Nanomaterial surface modification toolkit: Principles, components, recipes, and applications. *Advances in Colloid and Interface Science, 322*, 103035.

33. Ekinci, M.; Santos-Oliveira, R.; Ilem-Ozdemir, D. (2022).Biodistribution of 99mTc-PLA/PVA/Atezolizumab nanoparticles for non-small cell lung cancer diagnosis.*Eur. J. Pharm. Biopharm., 176*, 21–31.

34. Ekinci, M., Santos-Oliveira, R., & Ilem-Ozdemir, D. (2022). Biodistribution of 99mTc-PLA/PVA/Atezolizumab nanoparticles for non-small cell lung cancer diagnosis. *European Journal of Pharmaceutics and Biopharmaceutics, 176*, 21-31.

35. Ansari, M. T., Ramlan, T. A., Jamaluddin, N. N., Zamri, N., Salfi, R., Khan, A., ... & Hasnain, M. S. (2020). Lipid-based nanocarriers for cancer and tumor treatment. *Current pharmaceutical design, 26*(34), 4272-4276.

36. Deng, L., Xu, Y., Sun, C., Yun, B., Sun, Q., Zhao, C., & Li, Z. (2018). Functionalization of small black phosphorus nanoparticles for targeted imaging and photothermal therapy of cancer. *Science bulletin, 63*(14), 917-924.

37. Karch, A. (2017). Global, regional, and national burden of neurological disorders during 1990-2015: a systematic analysis for the Global Burden of Disease Study 2015.

38. Baccarini, C. I., Simon, M. W., Brandon, D., Christensen, S., Jordanov, E., & Dhingra, M. S. (2020). Safety and immunogenicity of a quadrivalent meningococcal conjugate vaccine in healthy meningococcal-naive children 2–9 years of age: a phase III, randomized study. *The Pediatric Infectious Disease Journal, 39*(10), 955-960.

39. Hansson, S. F., Andreasson, U., Wall, M., Skoog, I., Andreasen, N., Wallin, A., ... & Blennow, K. (2009). Reduced levels of amyloid-β-binding proteins in cerebrospinal fluid from Alzheimer's disease patients. *Journal of Alzheimer's disease, 16*(2), 389-397.

40. Jablonski, M. R., Markandaiah, S. S., Jacob, D., Meng, N. J., Li, K., Gennaro, V., ... & Pasinelli, P. (2014). Inhibiting drug efflux transporters improves efficacy of ALS therapeutics. *Annals of clinical and translational neurology, 1*(12), 996-1005.

41. Graverini, G., Piazzini, V., Landucci, E., Pantano, D., Nardiello, P., Casamenti, F., ... & Bergonzi, M. C. (2018). Solid lipid nanoparticles for delivery of andrographolide across

the blood-brain barrier: in vitro and in vivo evaluation. *Colloids and Surfaces B: Biointerfaces, 161*, 302-313.

42. Chae, S. H., & Lee, Y. H. (2014). Carbon nanotubes and graphene towards soft electronics. *Nano Convergence, 1*, 1-26.

43. Silva, G. A., Czeisler, C., Niece, K. L., Beniash, E., Harrington, D. A., Kessler, J. A., & Stupp, S. I. (2004). Selective differentiation of neural progenitor cells by high-epitope density nanofibers. *Science, 303*(5662), 1352-1355.

44. Sivaramakrishnan, S. M., & Neelakantan, P. (2014). Nanotechnology in dentistry-what does the future hold in store. *Dentistry, 4*(2), 1.

45. Lanza, G. M., Trousil, R. L., Wallace, K. D., Rose, J. H., Hall, C. S., Scott, M. J., ... & Wickline, S. A. (1998). In vitro characterization of a novel, tissue-targeted ultrasonic contrast system with acoustic microscopy. *The Journal of the Acoustical Society of America, 104*(6), 3665-3672.

46. Zhang, W., Wang, Y., Lee, B. T. K., Liu, C., Wei, G., & Lu, W. (2014). A novel nanoscale-dispersed eye ointment for the treatment of dry eye disease. *Nanotechnology, 25*(12), 125101.

47. Vadlapudi, A. D., CholKAr, K., Dasari, S. R., & Mitra, A. K. (2015). Ocular drug delivery. *Drug Deliv. Jones Bartlett Learn. Burlingt. Ma USA, 1*, 219-263.

48. Drug Deliv, Jones & Bartlett Learning, Burlington, MA, USA. 219-263

49. Popov, A. (2020). Mucus-penetrating particles and the role of ocular mucus as a barrier to micro-and nanosuspensions. *Journal of Ocular Pharmacology and therapeutics, 36*(6), 366-375.

50. Haleem, A., Javaid, M., Singh, R. P., Rab, S., & Suman, R. (2023). Applications of nanotechnology in medical field: a brief review. *Global Health Journal, 7*(2), 70-77.

51. Stoica, A. E., Chircov, C., & Grumezescu, A. M. (2020). Nanomaterials for wound dressings: an up-to-date overview. *Molecules, 25*(11), 2699.

52. Sahoo, S. K., Dilnawaz, F., & Krishnakumar, S. (2008). Nanotechnology in ocular drug delivery. *Drug discovery today, 13*(3-4), 144-151.

53. Amirtharaj Mosas, K. K., Chandrasekar, A. R., Dasan, A., Pakseresht, A., & Galusek, D. (2022). Recent advancements in materials and coatings for biomedical implants. *Gels, 8*(5), 323.

54. Giri, G., Maddahi, Y., & Zareinia, K. (2021). A brief review on challenges in design and development of nanorobots for medical applications. *Applied Sciences, 11*(21), 10385.

55. Yanik, M. F., Cinar, H., Cinar, H. N., Chisholm, A. D., Jin, Y., & Ben-Yakar, A. (2004). Functional regeneration after laser axotomy. *Nature, 432*(7019), 822-822.

56. Ali, A., Petrů, M., Azeem, M., Noman, T., Masin, I., Amor, N., ... & Tomková, B. (2023). A comparative performance of antibacterial effectiveness of copper and silver coated textiles. *Journal of Industrial Textiles, 53*, 15280837221134990.

57. Li, H., Yan, W., Suo, X., Peng, H., Yang, X., Li, Z., ... & Liu, D. (2019). Nucleus-targeted nano delivery system eradicates cancer stem cells by combined thermotherapy and hypoxia-activated chemotherapy. *Biomaterials, 200*, 1-14.

58. Adams, D., Gonzalez-Duarte, A., O'Riordan, W. D., Yang, C. C., Ueda, M., Kristen, A. V., ... & Suhr, O. B. (2018). Patisiran, an RNAi therapeutic, for hereditary transthyretin amyloidosis. *New england journal of medicine, 379*(1), 11-21.

59. Akinc, A., Maier, M. A., Manoharan, M., Fitzgerald, K., Jayaraman, M., Barros, S., ... & Cullis, P. R. (2019). The Onpattro story and the clinical translation of nanomedicines containing nucleic acid-based drugs. *Nature nanotechnology, 14*(12), 1084-1087.

60. Reddy, S., Malarvizhi, D., Venkatesh, A., & Vivekanandhan, P. (2020). Nanotechnology and its application in restorative dentistry: A review of literature. *Indian Journal of Forensic Medicine & Toxicology, 14*(4), 1215-1220.

61. Ventola, C. L. (2017). Progress in nanomedicine: approved and investigational nanodrugs. P T 42, 742–755.

62. He, H., Liu, L., Morin, E. E., Liu, M., & Schwendeman, A. (2019). Survey of clinical translation of cancer nanomedicines—lessons learned from successes and failures. *Accounts of chemical research, 52*(9), 2445-2461.

63. Sun, D., Zhou, S. and Gao, W. (2020). What went wrong with anticancer nanomedicine design and how to make it right. ACS Nano. 14:12281–90.

64. Souza, R. C. D., Haberbeck, L. U., Riella, H. G., Ribeiro, D. H., & Carciofi, B. A. (2019). Antibacterial activity of zinc oxide nanoparticles synthesized by solochemical process. *Brazilian Journal of Chemical Engineering, 36*(2), 885-893.